EVERYBODY NEEDS A

COACH

IN

LIFE

Isn't It Time You Found Yours?

MICHEAL BURT
The Super Coach

A SAVIO REPUBLIC BOOK
An Imprint of Post Hill Press

Everybody Needs a Coach in Life:
Isn't It Time You Found Yours?
© 2019 by Micheal J. Burt
All Rights Reserved
First Savio Republic Hardcover Edition: March 2017

ISBN: 978-1-64293-401-4
ISBN (eBook): 978-1-68261-161-6

Excerpts are from THE HOLY BIBLE, NEW INTERNATIONAL VERSION®, NIV®
Copyright © 1973, 1978, 1984, 2011 by Biblica, Inc.™ Used by permission.
All rights reserved worldwide.

Cover Design by Quincy Avilio
Interior Design and Composition by Greg Johnson/Textbook Perfect

Published in the United States of America

DEDICATION

Dedicating this book was easy. To my wife Natalie, who walked into one of my workshops and fell in love with her own potential. In the process, I fell in love with you.

To our beautiful daughter Ella Grace. I'm crying as I write this on a plane headed to speak and missing you every second. You inspire me more than you'll ever know. I need more of your lack of fear and energy.

I want both of you to see me reaching for my God-given potential and always playing offense versus defense.

To my mother Melanie Mayo, who had me when she was 16 years old. I've watched you scratch and claw for everything you've ever gotten. It rubbed off on me.

To my younger brother Dustin. Life hasn't always handed you a great deck of cards but you've always played them the best way you can. I'm proud of you brother. You get up every day and make it happen.

ACKNOWLEDGEMENTS

Every book you write brings more clarity about what your life's message really is. This is my biggest book to date and it encompasses what I believe at my core: that a good coach can change your life. A good coach will find and fill your missing structures. Each of the people below does that for me on a consistent basis.

I'd like to offer a special thank-you and gratitude to:

- ▶ My wife Natalie for always believing in me and steering me toward God's vision for us.
- ▶ My daughter Ella Grace for reminding me what potential is and for a spirit that touches my soul.
- ▶ My mother Melanie Mayo for teaching me to finish what I start and see something through to its logical conclusion.
- ▶ My father James Burt for helping me to remember to have fun along the journey.
- ▶ My good friend Tommy Davidson for being a sounding board for my big ideas and being my biggest coaching success story of my entire career.
- ▶ My agent Nena Madonia for urging me to write this book after listening to my convictions.
- ▶ My friends Grant Cardone, Matt Manero, and Brad Lea for inspiring me to "Be Obsessed vs. Be Average."
- ▶ My team in Brandon Ray and Takisha Bromell for helping to scale our company and create great engagement with our clients.
- ▶ My driver Teddy Taylor for getting me to and from all my speaking engagements and reminding me what true grit and hard work is all about.

- ▶ My Monster Producers for offering me the ability to work with big-time business builders every month.
- ▶ My pastor Brady Cooper for including my talents in the church and being my spiritual mentor.
- ▶ My good friend Tom Love for creating and sharing the "explanation of services" with me and through me to the world.

I believe we all have a song to sing and people to sing it too. I hope this book encourages you to write the book of your life as well.

CONTENTS

PREFACE

Tim Ferris, best-selling author of *The 4-Hour Workweek in a podcast*, once said, "Every bit of a man's confidence can be traced back to one of two things: a woman who walked into his life or a coach who believed in him and changed it." He was spot on. I too believe a good coach can change your life and it is typically a good woman who helps a man get his swag back. Too many people, however, will not accept a coach's help, because of pride, insecurity, complacency, or they just don't really know what a good coach can do for them or why they need one. Consequently, these people will keep repeating their past patterns of mistakes, drastically handicapping their bigger futures, and they don't even know it. Time after time, they will make these cycles of mistakes, sometimes for years and sometimes over a lifetime. Too many people endure a life of underachievement, stifled impact in the world, and subpar performance.

I believe within everyone is a song to sing and there is an audience to sing it to. However, people just don't know how to find the song inside them or how to get it out in a meaningful way. They don't know how to find what makes them unique, don't know how to package what makes them unique, and more important, don't know how to capitalize on what makes them unique through packaging. This is true even for some of the top performers in the world who are still undercapitalized. There is still an enormous gap between their achievements and the incredible unharnessed potential inside them.

As a coach to as many as a thousand people in a week, I see several ways people don't fully utilize their talents. You have extraordinary gifts but you may be using them in very ordinary ways. I believe you were hardwired by the Creator to influence the world in bigger and more meaningful ways but for some reason, you've relegated yourself to the monotonous and trivial, repeating the patterns of the past and leaving your potential on the table. Fortunately, you can change this pattern. Even the best face boredom, insecurity, or uncertainty about their future; I see it on their faces and in their actions when I'm speaking or coaching them. That is the moment they need a catalyst so they're able to take action and do something new or different to bust through that one ceiling they can't seem to bust through.

As I write this in an airport in Cancun, Mexico, I just finished a two-day coaching session with 25 financial advisors who earn more than $1 million per year. *They are tired, bored, and ready to retire.* However, after just two days, even they saw the value of having someone challenge them to push harder to close the gap between their current performance and their potential. After spending less than a day with me, many were ready to go back to work and revive their careers and impact. They were ready to engage vs. dis-engage. They just needed a coach to walk into their lives and speak to their unlimited potential. They just needed a coach.

My mother always told me that the very day my grandfather "retired" and was no longer active as as a cabinet maker, home builder, entrepreneur, and hustler, his health begin to disintegrate. An estimated 40% of people are depressed when they retire because there is no purpose that drags them out of bed, nothing to look forward to, nothing to fight for. The biblical story of David was of a great man of God as long as he was in the battle and engaged with his work, but when he stayed home and watched the "Bathsheba show on the internet," his life fell apart. When he dis-engaged he shut down and so did his blessing. With time on his hands and no battle to fight he wandered into trouble. I like to look at life in one of three states at all times:

1. Dynamic and growing, which means alive and prospering.
2. Static and stuck which means stagnant and plateaued.
3. Entropic, which means slow disintegration or dying. An airplane is always ascending and climbing, plateaued at flying altitude, or descending. Our lives are the same way.

This book will show that no matter how successful you are, the career choices you've made or the life path you've taken, YOU need a good coach who will challenge you from various angles in all dimensions of your life. I believe this book can become that coach.

When you get uncomfortable (which is a necessary step if you're going to expand), you'll contract and retreat. You'll digress, not progress. You'll never push through the discomfort without the help of an expert who can show you why you're making missteps and how you can change. Every Olympian, every actor, every great CEO, and every professional athlete has a coach. Professionals in any arena know that they bring bias, assumption, and prejudgment to every scenario. That is why they want someone to offer an objective view of their life, career, and business. They yearn to bust through the ceiling and recognize they cannot do it on their own.

Just as the keen observer Tim Ferris predicted, it was two people who changed my life. A woman gave me back my confidence when I had lost every bit of it after a miserable and debilitating breakup when I was in my twenties. It was a coach who helped me to believe that one day I could impact millions. Both people walked into my life and opened my eyes to things I never even imagined. *This book will awaken you from the slumber you've been in and help you break through the limits you've encountered in your life.* This book will tackle all three of the major problems that hold people back that I see, which are:

1. **You don't know what to do so your confidence is low and you are just floundering.** Insecure people who have this problem always contract and retreat to a place of comfort and complacency. They live in a state of frustration but are unable to take action. Even the most successful people can find themselves in this position, uncertain what to do next or how to continue to create a larger vision and mountain to climb.

2. **You know what to do and you've done it well, but you've hit a plateau and can't quite figure out how to break through that plateau.** You work harder and harder but get the same results, leaving you tired and discouraged. You are static but successful. You are living the American Dream but sometimes it feels like a nightmare. You want more but can't seem to get more. Breaking through doesn't require monumental steps but small changes can bring dramatic results.

3. **You have mastered and conquered your craft but you are now incredibly bored and yearning for a greater pursuit, calling, and influence.** Success in many ways

has lost its meaning so you feel numb. Sometimes the smarter or more advanced we become the more intellectually lazy we get. Fortunately, you can learn to awaken and realize the "unattended dreams" in your life. This book will show you how to attack that "success comfort" you're facing so you can commit to leading a life of impact and significance.

A good coach will challenge you. A good coach will kick you in the butt when you need it and pat you on the back when it's deserving. I encourage you to be open, humble, hungry, and coachable and take this journey with me. I'll uncover that hidden potential in you, just as I did for more than a decade as a Hall of Fame women's basketball coach. You'll start reading quietly but you'll finish the book as a dynamo. You'll be transformed in ways you never even imagined. You'll wake up and recognize there is a bigger future for you. You'll be motivated and inspired to take incredible steps. You'll rekindle your inner fire.

And that, my friend, is why I have written this book. I have a burning desire to spread the message that "Everybody Needs a Coach in Life" to all 7 billion people on Planet Earth, and possibly even to the few on Mars.

INTRODUCTION

No one disputes that we're living in "the current of the urgent" where people are asked to do more, give more, and become more. There's a seemingly endless stream of voice mails, tweets, Facebook messages, invites on LinkedIn, Snapchats, e-mails, and more confronting everyone. The result? People simply don't know how to give more, don't have the motivation to give it, can't sort through the clutter, or don't have the confidence to bridge the gap between what they know or want to do and what they actually do. This breeds a vicious cycle you're going to hear about a great deal in this book of ***starting with good intentions, failing to follow through for a variety of reasons, then an ensuing guilt*** about our lost potential before we hit the repeat button again. This is the precise reason you need a coach; they will help you break this vicious cycle. Success in one role doesn't justify failure in another. The challenge is that people want to accomplish as much as they can but their lives have gotten so complicated that they're stuck. They're restless. When they do get a minute of quite and reflective time they yearn for more impact. They need to find someone to help *take the complicated life and make it simple*, both in their personal and professional lives.

The high achievers need to be challenged so they don't get bored; the average need to be coached so they can reach a higher level of play; and the trailing performers need to be pushed in another direction where they are more likely to succeed. There is no time to waste. We need a sense of urgency. As I said in one of my earlier books, *"This Ain't No Practice Life."* Too many individuals have talents, passion, and conscience but don't have the discipline to activate their natural abilities and as a result, won't achieve their true potential. Others may be "producing" at high levels but are, in fact, close to burnout. At best, most of us operate in a mechanical mode, which is a fancy way of saying "we are just surviving." This model is not sustainable and will end in disaster personally or professionally.

With all of life's stress and complexities, I believe it is necessary to have someone who can help you find clarity, focus, structure, and confidence. This is why I believe we are in the middle of a "Coaching Revolution." Soon, every manager in America will need coaching skills and every athletic coach will need business acumen and the ability to connect to the ***body, mind, heart, and spirit*** of their players to activate all their potential, and every parent will need to be a great coach to their children. I'm not exaggerating. I believe that everyone's future potential is at stake. If people are unable to fulfill their potential, invent what is deep inside of them, make breakthrough medical and scientific discoveries . . . and more, then we all face a much sadder and unproductive future. Critical thinker Randy Gage once said in his book *Mad Genius*, "Nothing dumbs down and dampens creativity like wasting it in the pursuit of mediocrity."

I have an uncompromising belief that a good coach can change your life. I also believe a bad coach squanders good talent. You have seen it at every level, from junior pro basketball to the NBA or NFL. A coach takes the raw and undeveloped potential and turns it into something recognizable. He converts low-level players into high-achievers who can produce.

In this "Coaching Revolution" I talk about how you fall into one of three categories:

1. *You are a coach; you see yourself as someone who develops talents in others in a consistent way.* You are genuinely interested in developing the talent in others which will take effort on your part. Not all are interested in anything outside of their own personal success. They don't want to coach or develop the talent in anyone.

2. *You are being coached and you are hungry, humble, and teachable.* You show up with a learner's spirit and always get something out of everything. You have no pre-judgment and are looking for an unfair advantage through your education.

3. *You just don't want a coach; you are closed off, narrow minded, and stuck.*

If you're in the third group, I pity you because you're going to stagnate and become obsolete in the competitive business arena and will probably be replaced by someone who is hungry, humble, and teachable. You most likely didn't fall in to that third group or you would not have picked up this book. Remember, you are either dynamic, static, or entropic. If you're not growing, you're just slowly diminishing and ultimately dying. Group three is "living with the dead." Dead energy. Dead mindsets. Dead futures. They will most likely never get any new results greater than what they've gotten in the past. You will hear them use words like stuck, stagnant or "in a rut."

I believe your competitive advantage comes from either your past packaged in a way that is useful for solving problems, or the coach whom you choose to help you take your talents to the world in an accelerated and differentiated manner. ***Who coaches you matters more than you think.*** Your past, combined with a skilled expert who can accelerate your skill sets, can lead to uncovering your ENTIRE competitive advantage, and in a saturated and commoditized world that advantage is critical to winning. Imagine if I was interviewing for a job and said that I was personally coached by Tony Robbins, Nick Saban, or John Wooden or I was an apprentice to Jack Welch or Andrew Carnegie. Do you believe this would give me a competitive advantage in the market? Of course it would. On the other hand, if you wandered through job after job with no clear direction, no coaching, and no guidance, you wouldn't have a competitive advantage. You would be left settling for the crumbs left behind because all the good stuff would have been taken by the people who had been coached.

I've organized this book in such a way that, like a coach, it helps you identify your missing structures, which is a void, gap, or hole that needs to be filled if you plan on moving to a new level. For some their missing structure is just energy. They live in isolation with their thoughts, ideas, and actions and this excludes them from bigger futures. This book walks you through systems that will bring clarity to your chaos. It forces you to take a hard look at your entire life including aspects that you haven't examined in years or have put on autopilot. It questions every assumption you have. It outlines strategies for breakthroughs. It shows you how to coach others and how to build effective teams in today's "free agent nation."

My message is simple: Everybody needs a coach in life. Isn't it about time you found yours? Start reading!

1

A GOOD COACH
CAN CHANGE YOUR LIFE

Wayne Dyer used to tell a story of how before he was born; he had a conversation with God and God asked him what he wanted to be when he grew up. Wayne thought and thought and finally said, "I'd like to be the number one person in the world who teaches self-reliance." God then said, "Are you sure you want this to be your life's mission during your time on Earth?" Wayne responded, "Yes, I do." God thought for a minute and then said, "Well then, Wayne, I'll give you a father that is an alcoholic who will walk out on you and your family very early in life. You'll never see him and he will abdicate all of his parental responsibilities. Your mother will be incapable of raising you and your brothers and you will be given over to a foster home. Throughout a series of these stays in multiple orphanages, you will learn what it really means to be self-reliant. You will become somewhat of a coach to the other kids because of your mind-set and internal instincts. This will become your training ground for your future assignment and one day you will be considered the greatest self-reliance guru in the world." When Wayne Dyer passed from this earth at age of 75, he was considered one of the greatest self-help and self-reliance teachers in the world, and had sold an estimated 60 million books. I believe God created coaches because he knew that people couldn't reach their potential on their own.

I, too, believe I had a conversation with God before I was born, and I told him I wanted to be a coach. It's the only thing that would explain why I've devoted my entire life to helping to unlock the potential in others.

The burning desire of coaches to help develop other people's potential comes from a seed planted early in life. Becoming a world-class coach starts by "being turned on to something by somebody." Backtrack your journey and tell me it didn't start with you being enlightened to something by somebody in your life. You may or may not have personally known that person but something they did, said, or modeled made you feel a certain way and you wanted more of that feeling. My mother had me when she was 16 years old and my father, 18, was not much older. They were just kids who probably conceived me with little or no plans for the future. They quickly married mostly, I believe, because my grandfather forced them to, but the marriage didn't last long. I have little to no recollection of early childhood except for how hard my mother worked for what we did have (which was very little), how little my father was involved, and my babysitters, including both grandmothers, aunts and uncles on both sides of the family, and my Head Start teachers. I could tell they all believed at some level that I had the makings of something special, and I always felt special. When Steve Jobs felt unloved by his adopted parents they assured him that they chose him because he was special and hand selected. All of those in my life made me feel the same way, that I was put on Earth to impact people in a special way. I now try to affirm this in my four-year-old daughter so she knows her life has a purpose. *In a way, all those baby sitters represented my early coaches in life*. They ingrained in me the basics from good and bad, survival and competition, scarcity and abundance, and dreams and realities.

The word admonition means "strong, life-changing counsel." As I look back on my early life that's exactly what some of my early coaches gave me. They each played a pivotal role in shaping me that persists to this day. Some of that scripting has turned out to be opposite of my beliefs. I have had to re-wire the scarcity that was ingrained in early my life to accept abundance. Without coaches like these in our lives, we will always revert to comfort, complacency, and the path of least resistance. It's our nature to retreat rather than shoot for the moon. Without structures and guidance from people other than your parents, you grow up to become self-absorbed, unaware of how interdependent the world is and how you can combine your talents with others to create something far bigger together than working on your own. Lacking a coach stunts your emotional growth, skill sets, and ability to bounce back from adversity. I see many good kids who don't have much confidence, can't see their bigger futures, or lack the drive to attain what they want. That's because they don't have someone in their life who believes in them or will push them to be accountable to a bigger dream. They just wander and underperform; their potential won't be realized and chances are they won't leave their mark on the world the way they were supposed to.

By the time I was age six, my mother was taking me to the ball field to hone my social and athletic skills. It was there that I uncovered my "birthday gifts," which for me was the ability to see the whole and the parts and how they interconnected with each other to create a perfect union. Even at six my coach could see my ability to lead, squeeze out potential in myself and others, and encourage others. Birthday gifts are the set of unique skills and talents hardwired in you at birth by the Creator, that must be found, nurtured, and refined throughout your life. Take a minute and think about your birthday gifts. Most adults believe that their gifts are simply the following:

- ▸ I'm a good person.
- ▸ I work hard.
- ▸ I show up on time.
- ▸ I'm a people person.

I hate to tell you but these are not "birthday gifts." Those are attributes. This book will help you decipher your true skills, those that you can use to solve real problems and be paid to teach others. The sooner we recognize these gifts in ourselves and in our children the faster we will accelerate our ability to do wonderful and inspiring things.

For me it was one particular coach, a woman named Micki Vinson, who walked into my life and changed it forever. She was one of my first coaches, and had a tremendous impact on me. I remember as if it was yesterday when she said directly to me in front of the other kids, "Son, one of these days you're going to become a coach." She spoke validation and vision into my life. Vision is the bridge between the present and the future. The Bible says without it we perish or go "unrestrained." Think of all of the times in your life that you have gone "unrestrained" because you couldn't cultivate a vision or no one spoke a vision into your life. That day, you would have thought the clouds opened up and a ray of sunshine from God was shining directly down on that moment of clarity. Micki did for me what good coaches always do: *They affirm and validate the worth and potential in you in such a way that you begin to see it in your own self, even when your self-confidence is so low you don't even believe it yourself.*

Now don't miss this. Lots of people are on the wrong bus in life. I believe it's clear why. In life, many times we end up pursuing a field because we were "turned on to something by somebody" but what if we didn't have that person who turned us on and made sure we saw something through to its logical conclusion? I encourage you to backtrack to a day in your life when someone you trusted and respected said these four very powerful words to you, "I believe in you." Have you turned away from some of your original visions or some dream in your heart that you haven't had the confidence to pursue? Unfortunately, today we rarely take the time to speak vision into each other anymore, in our homes, with our friends, to our children, and especially not in the workplace. Our competitive society is built on transaction, struggle, scarcity, and fear. We're overworked, overstressed, overtaxed, and overcomplicated. We need people in our lives who take the complicated and make it simple. We need people in our lives who sow in us, not take energy from us. We need people who will speak a vision into our lives as Micki did for me. That one vision and affirmation statement would lead me to my life's work and ultimate calling in life. A good coach affirms and validates the vision, which, if fueled by energy, becomes manifested in life.

Dan Sullivan, one of my coaches, coined the term Unique ability®, which means "some superior ability usually given to us at a very early age that when honed and perfected separates us from others in our field." This ability is typically recognized by others and rewarded in the form of love, affirmation, reputation, appreciation, referrals and, lastly money. (I believe money is only a byproduct of value creation and problems solved with our specific talents or processes.) Once you decipher how your unique talents can solve problems for others, then the work will seem effortless because it aligns your natural talent with your vocation. This is the difference between an occupation and collecting a paycheck and fulfilling a calling in life. My Unique ability® that Micki was sensing was that I thought like a coach. I analyzed like a coach. I pushed like a coach. I inherited a very valuable trait from my father: I could talk to and relate to everyone. I saw what others could become and pushed them to become it, whether they believed it or not. Sometimes as a coach I pushed too hard; I was once ejected from a junior pro basketball game with three technical fouls given to me by one of my best friends. Nevertheless, I still received a standing ovation on the way out because, while people didn't like my competitive spirit, they could sense my passion.

I believe my coaching acumen was hardwired in to me by God and then honed very early in life by people who recognized this gift in me. However, what if no one spoke that belief or vision into me when I was young? Then my vision would just be "unrestrained" and most likely I wouldn't have found my calling and probably wouldn't have had such a productive life. When you don't find your "manufactured gifts," you spend life bouncing from place to place and job to job and don't have much impact on the people around you or the world at large. When you don't find this "voice," you wake up and solve very small problems and are rewarded in the form of love, money, and appreciation in very small ways. I often say, "You can't put 50 cents into a dollar coke machine and get a dollar coke out. What you put in, you get back. "The world rewards you for using your gifting. What happens when we don't find our unique gifting and talents? In the book of Matthew 25:14–30 here is the parable of the talents:

"For it will be like a man going on a journey, who called his servants[a] and entrusted to them his property.[15] To one he gave five talents,[b] to another two, to another one, to each according to his ability. Then he went away.[16] He who had received the five talents went at once and traded with them, and he made five talents more.[17] So also he who had the two talents made two talents more.[18] But he who had received the one talent went and dug in the ground and hid his master's money.[19] Now after a long time the master of those servants came and settled accounts with them.[20] And he who had received the five talents came forward, bringing five talents more, saying, 'Master, you delivered to me five talents; here I have made five talents more.'[21] His master said to him, 'Well done, good and faithful servant.[c] You have been faithful over a little; I will set you over much. Enter into the joy of your master.'[22] And he also who had the two talents came forward, saying, 'Master, you delivered to me two talents; here I have made two talents more.'[23] His master said to him, 'Well done, good and faithful servant. You have been faithful over a little; I will set you over much. Enter into the joy of your master.'[24] He also who had received the one talent came forward, saying, 'Master, I knew you to be a hard man, reaping where you did not sow, and gathering where you scattered no seed,[25] so I was afraid, and I went and hid your talent in the ground. Here you have what is yours.'[26] But his master answered him, 'You wicked and slothful servant! You knew that I reap where I have not sown and gather where I scattered no seed?[27] Then you ought to have invested my money with the bankers, and at my coming I should have received what was my own with interest.[28] So take the talent from him and give it to him who has the ten talents.[29] For to everyone who has will more be given, and he will have an abundance. But from the one who has not, even what he has will be taken away.[30] And cast the worthless servant into the outer darkness. In that place there will be weeping and gnashing of teeth.'

Notice how the story ends, "For to everyone who has will more be given, and he will have an abundance. But from the one who has not, even what he has will be taken away. And cast the worthless servant into the outer darkness. In that place there will be weeping and gnashing of teeth."

For the ones who took the talents and multiplied them they heard this, "Well done, good and faithful servant. You have been faithful over a little; I will set you over much. Enter into the joy of your master."

For the one who hid the talent out of scarcity here was the message, "You wicked and slothful servant! You knew that I reap where I have not sown and gather where I scattered no seed?[27] Then you ought to have invested my money with the bankers, and at my coming I should have received what was my own with interest.[28] So take the talent from him and give it to him who has the ten talents." This message is pretty clear. We should take whatever talent we have been given and seek to grow or multiply it. This implies first that we find our talent and then utilize it. Many have never found theirs and some who have found it are not utilizing it.

If we can help children find their hardwired gifts early and then nourish and nurture them, there would be more happiness and less hopelessness and struggle. Studies show the average 20- to 30-year-old will change jobs as much as 24 to 37 times over his or her lifetime. I believe this trend is because they **have not found their voice or opened their birthday gifts.** That is because they don't have a coach, or possibly are not receptive to being coached. A good coach helps you discover and act on your factory-installed talents. A good coach accelerates your gifts. A good coach finds and helps you fill your missing structures. Often, you don't even know what those missing structures are and need an outsider to help identify them.

At many of my training sessions, I ask people to outline the pivot points they have experienced over their lives. They can easily diagram them and show both the positive and negative game-changing moments. Typically, these moments occurred because someone took a personal interest in their success even when the individuals didn't appreciate the contribution or impact they were making. When I was age 15, two critical pivot points took place. A local dentist told me I should run for a National Beta Club office, where I would give speeches and lead other young people all over the country. In addition, a local junior pro coach asked me to help him coach a junior pro basketball team. I believed I could do the latter but didn't believe I could be a public speaker. Remember what I've said: *A good coach will push you to do things you never believed you could do*, and the coach will take great pride watching your achieve what you believed was impossible. Is it any surprise that today I speak and coach around the world using the skills these coaches helped me find?

I suspect that less than 20% of people have married their talents with their work. Undoubtedly, that's why there are so many frustrated and unsatisfied people in the world. You may appear to be very successful outwardly but actually feel very unfulfilled. You may be satisfied briefly when you're successful but you won't be truly happy and fulfilled if you're not using your true calling. Too many people spend most of their life at a job they don't love and wish they could have more. ***God designed you for a purpose.*** You were "factory installed" by the manufactuer for greatness. You were made to grow and expand and prosper and take dominion of your area of expertise. You were not made to have a spirit of timidity or fear but rather of abudance and action.

There are millions of people who are either burned out or in mechanical mode, grinding away and feeling overwhelmed.

They can't find the lever to pull to scale their business, create more income, or take their big dreams and make them come to fruition. Although they may appear successful, they're actually frustrated.

You would be hard-pressed to find a top CEO, top performer, top athlete, or top Olympian who doesn't turn to a coach to help take their insecurities and confusion and turn them into crystallized clarity. Even Steve Jobs took a walk with his coach every Sunday to bounce ideas, get counsel, and share strategies.

With a great coach, your dormant forces and faculties become alive. Your latent and underdeveloped skills awaken and you do things you never believed possible. Like a fly fisherman who wears polarized glasses to help him see the fish underwater, a good coach has *trained eyes* to pinpoint where you need the most help. Remember, you can't see the picture when you are inside the frame. You just keep hitting the repeat button and doing the same old tired things repeatedly, leaving you feeling hopeless and confused. You need another person to hold you accountable to your own dreams. You need another person to believe in you when you don't even believe in yourself.

What You Need Is a Good Coach

But, first consider what happens when you have a bad coach? Sometimes I start my presentations off with this question, "How many of you have ever had a bad coach in life?" People laugh and almost EVERYONE raises their hands. They think back to one person who cost them time, energy, and their future. I say, "So you know the cost in terms of your squandered potential when you had that bad coach?" Everyone acknowledges that it was a miserable period where they had little or no faith in their leader, a poor one-sided relationship, and a lack of fulfillment of talent, both collectively as a unit and individually. But can you still learn from a bad coach? Of course, you learn what not to do! I would never want my child to play for one if I could help it. I also would never want my child to work for a bad manager. A poor manager wastes good talent and crushes the spirit of employees, leaving behind a culture of malaise. When this happens, the employees feel there are only two ways to respond:

1. The employees want to hurt the manager so they rebel or quit, maliciously obey, or willingly comply.

2. They just check out. They still show up physically but essentially they quite because their spirit, mind, and heart is no longer there. In essence they quit, but they forgot to tell anybody.

At age 16, my teammates and I were introduced to a former University of Tennessee basketball player from East Tennessee named Seth McDonald. Seth was determined to come into our little town and whip a group of subpar athletes into shape and build a basketball program. I admired his drive but couldn't connect to his philosophy. Apparently, no one else could either. From day one it was a disaster for everyone. He didn't understand how to win the players or the community over to his side of thinking and fought with virtually everybody, including the girls' coach, all the time. People ridiculed him, parents hated him, and nothing he tried worked. I never completely sold out to Coach McDonald, and that's a shame because it cost both of us lost years and potential we can't get back. He had my body but never connected with my mind, heart, or spirit. He always told me I was "too slow" but seldom told me how to fix the problem or improve my confidence. On the other hand, a good coach offers specific strategies to minimize your liabilities and enhance your assets instead of simply saying you have a problem. *You know you have a problem, that's why you need the coach.* What we need is less theory and more how to. The funny thing was that I called Coach McDonald many years later when I became a head coach because of one reason: he never sold out either. No matter how many times that man went in front of the school board to discuss his fate he always stood tall and never backed down. Although I thought he was a poor coach who never connected with his team, I walked away with some backbone of my own. Many years later when I was tested, falsely accused of stealing money from the booster club, and investigated by the department of children's services for working players too hard (I was found innocent), I always kept my backbone. It turns out that I learned quite a bit from that bad coach which has served me well in life in every endeavor. I'll never forget that man.

At age 18, I walked into the elementary school I had attended and demanded to be the boys' head basketball coach. At first, the principal balked and said, "Son, you are just a kid. I could never make you the head boys' basketball coach here." Nevertheless, I went back there every day for two weeks. (I later learned that it typically takes between seven to fifteen touches to convert a prospect to a client.) I went back for 14 straight days to make my case, stress my passion and conviction, and show the principal that I was ready. He relented and offered me the job as long as another adult was with me all the time. In the first year I coached, we won a state championship (the only one in the school's history). By the way, I was paid a whopping $199.50 for the entire year.

I found my "calling" and would never look back again.

You may be wondering whether there is a difference between *coaching* and *consulting*. While similar in some ways, coaches take a more interactive approach with their clients. A consultant usually assesses client needs and then issues a report or recommendations, often leaving it up to the clients to figure out what to do. Coaches, on the other hand, focus on specifics—how you can find and fill structure and follow a new system. The coach will stay with you throughout the process because the coach's success is tied to your success. A coach has to manage many of the challenges of those he or she is coaching. The coach is akin to a strategist, motivator, psychologist, therapist, and innovator.

I want to clarify how training has evolved as well so you understand how different people can serve as your coaches. The definition of training is "engaging a person or group in a set of systematic and consistent behaviors that allows them to do something tomorrow they simply cannot do today." It is built on a trusting relationship between the player and the coach developed through their work and shared goals. However, most players prefer a quick fix and easy transformation. They want to read a book, attend a single session, or do something once. In fact, transformation typically only occurs when we are continually and persistently involved in something. This is why our current generation is referred to as the "microwave generation." Could a personal trainer be a coach? Yes. Could a speaker who has a unique methodology and works with people in a *consistent manner* to drive new results over a period of time be a coach? Yes. Could a mentor who "coaches" people through a shift in knowledge, skills, desire, confidence, likability, networks, or ways to penetrate the market or get new customers be a coach? Yes. Just remember a coach has followers and is driving people toward some dominant aspiration in life with a focus, an intention, and an intensity that will not stop. A coach has a unique skill set to help people to do, reach, strive, and accomplish.

Coaching involves more than asking questions. *It involves asking people to do something they haven't done before and think in new ways.* The coach can quickly find these gaps in a client's life or business and then prescribe the best course of action so the person can manifest a new direction. The strategy may be as simple as boosting someone's self-confidence or as complicated as providing a selling strategy or a growth model. I believe God created coaches because he knew that left to our own devices we will always take the path of least resistance.

At 19 years old, I became an assistant coach at the third largest high school in Tennessee. I quickly rose through the ranks to the top assistant spot and when my boss, a wonderful man named Keith Short, retired at age 52, he recommended me to succeed him. At age 22, I became the youngest head coach in the state. The school had more than 2,500 students and I was in for the ride of my life. I inherited a program that had won some and lost a lot. Only one time before in 1979 (this was 1999) had my team been in a championship game and the team lost. It would be my job to build a dynasty. We did it in nine years. In less than a decade, we had won over 220 games, four conference titles, three substate appearances, two Miss Basketball Finalist and one state championship. My team would go on to win five state championships in the next seven years including a USA Today National championship title.

From my experience, especially from building a winning basketball team, I learned a lot about human dynamics and growing teams and cultures that win time and time again. I would go on to call our program "The Greatness Factory" because we took people from all walks of life, all socio-economic backgrounds, and all talent levels and we "manufactured greatness."

I retired from my athletic coaching at age 31 to pursue a bigger calling. Part of that calling is writing this book and impacting millions of people around the world. I want you to start seeing your place of business as a "Greatness Factory" that takes raw material that is not always packaged up or ready to go and transforms it into greatness. People come to you with some knowledge, some skill, some effort, and some confidence. Because of you and your skill set you convert their low thoughts of value to high thoughts of value. You convert and transfer their energy. You "manufactuer their greatness."

Why I Believe Talent Is Overrated

Tiger Woods was raised by his retired father who had time to take his son (as young as seven months) to the golf course. Mozart was playing music at age two. Bill Gates went to work with his dad at age 11. Were these men so much more gifted than others or had they just found their voice much earlier in life and had someone they trusted pushing them to take their vision and manifest it into reality? Would you excel at something if you were able to practice day in and day out, year after year, for 20 consecutive years? If you subscribe to Malcolm Gladwell's theory in his book *The Tipping Point*, that most people experience a breakthrough at the 10-year mark, or after 10,000 hours of practice, you understand that focused talent in a concentrated area with recalibration and coaching from someone who is trained will make you exceptional. Would it surprise you that it was in my tenth year as a women's basketball coach that I won a championship? Moreover, that happened after 10,000 hours of practice, trying and doing, failing and re-calibrating, and winning and losing. It was also only after I sat down with six other championship coaches and asked what they were doing that I wasn't that I connected the dots—and made the 10% of change I needed to make to win the championship. That's proof of the all-important change theory: very small changes make a significant impact in my life. Those championship coaches coached me. They rebuked me. They challenged me. And some of them downright irritated me. However, everything they did worked. They convinced me to move away from some of my past strategies and shift gears. In fact, studies consistently show that people who are coached and trained outperform those who are not, often by as much as 37% to 43%. While in The Strategic Coaching Program™ with Dan Sullivan I doubled my income year over year. I may or may not have done that without the program's help but I'm fully convinced that this program accelerated my progress. It was the structure. It was the mind challenges. It was the exposure to others who opened my eyes and expanded my vision. It was up to me to place myself in these environments and invest the money in my greatest asset—my future.

I'm surprised that so many people don't see the need for a coach in their life. Think about the unhealthy and out-of-shape people you see "working out" at the gym compared to the people who are exercising with a trainer. I know my workouts when I'm alone aren't nearly as intense as when I'm working with my trainer. It is the coach who challenges us to do thinks that we don't think we can, especially when we're feeling discomfort or pain.

You probably are already working with coaches in your daily life although you may not be calling them coaches. Consider the roles the following people have:

- ▶ Pastors are trained to take the complexity out of the Bible and help us understand the word of God and to create more disciples through their teachings. This is why we go to church on Sundays and gather with other believers to study the word.

- ▶ Doctors are trained to find our health problems and prescribe remedies so we can get healthy quickly. They spend eight years in medical school to study so they can accelerate our well-being.

- ▶ Parents are inspired to teach their children better ways of living so the offspring will become successful contributing members of society. The more enlightened the parent, the stronger the skill set passed on to the children so they can avoid many of the pitfalls of their parents.

I believe good coaches take the complicated and make it simple. They bring us clarity where there is confusion. They instill confidence in us that we can't seem to find on our own. They believe in us when we want to quit. As children, our teachers serve as our coaches but once we reach adolescence, we rebel against someone "training us." Teens at that age tend to believe their way is the only way. This is a dangerous notion, especially if it persists into adulthood. There are simply areas of life in which we are not experts. Perhaps out of hubris, we begin to believe we are "above coaching." I once mentioned to a businessman that I wanted to work with the most elite in our community. His response to me was, "In all fairness, we are worth millions more dollars than you are. What are you going to teach us?" Financially I had very little to teach him but emotionally I could teach him a great deal. Just because someone earns more money that you do doesn't mean he has it together and can't learn anything from you. Although successful in one aspect of life, we can be total failures in others. My favorite author and coach, Dr. Stephen Covey, once said, "Success in one role of your life doesn't justify failure in another." I suspect I could learn a lot from my millionaire friend about finances just as he could learn a great deal about organization, structure, building effective teams, and interpersonal skills from me. The first step to having a coach is humility. You must realize that while you're content with your current success, you can work on other areas of your life. Recently, I decided that I wanted to dig deeper into the bible. I immediately went looking for advanced courses, teachers who could accelerate my growth, and conferences I could attend. I was READY. When the pupil is ready, the teacher shows up, right? The first step though, is a burning desire to dig in. This is the missing ingredient for many people.

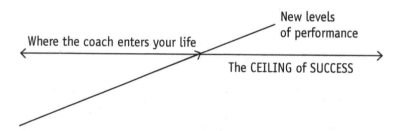

Until you see the need for a coach in your life, you'll most likely achieve some level of success, but I suspect that will come with a ceiling. You will repeatedly achieve certain levels of success but not exceed them until you decide to bring in a skilled expert who can elevate your performance.

It's time to do an inventory of areas in which you are hungry and see whether you're ready to grow or stagnate in that area.

What's Your Ceiling?

Just as every building has a ceiling, you too have one. It's an area of your life in which you have gone as far as YOU can go "on your own" with your insights, knowledge base, and skill sets. Humility is knowing you have the ceiling. Desire is wanting to bust through it.

When you recognize that you've hit your ceiling, it is time to call in the experts. This happens when:

1. You get the same number of wins every year by or the team finishes in the same place year after year.
2. You earn the same amount of money year after year even with increased work and stress.
3. You maintain the same amount of weight or body fat even though you go to the gym five days a week.
4. Your company has the same level of revenue despite trying double-digit strategies to improve it.
5. Your company has the same levels of profit even though the firm is growing in revenue.
6. You have the same level of happiness when you're achieving so much in life.
7. You have the same level of participation in your spiritual walk with the Lord without maturing into deeper discipline even though you attend church and worship on a regular basis.
8. You spend the same amount of energy with your loved ones even though you are trying to have a good amount of energy left over after a long day and not distribute crumbs to the ones you love the most.

9. You have the same level of energy even though you try different strategies throughout the day to improve your health.

10. You maintain the same level of bad habits you just can't seem to break no matter how hard you try.

We all have kryptonite. We all have blind spots. We all have parts of our life that just seem to stagnate because we go back and forth between the commitment to change and the actual effort it takes to achieve a new result. Remember *new results require new behavior. We can't meet a new stimulus with an old response.* What got us here won't get us there.

Medical experts say that a good plastic surgeon never makes more than seven changes and each change is never larger than 2.2 millimeters. These small but critical changes can yield major results. (We discuss this in greater detail in chapter 4.) For now, let us examine your life and ask what ceilings you have reached in four core areas:

1. **Body:** I've hit a ceiling in this area of my physical appearance. I need coaching because I'm not happy with my appearance.

2. **Mind:** I've hit a ceiling in this area of knowledge. I'm eager to grow in my mind because I need a new knowledge base to get to the next level.

3. **Heart:** I've hit a ceiling in the emotional level of my life or relationship. I need help because I'm lukewarm or passive in my most important relationships or my work.

4. **Spirit:** I've hit a ceiling in my spiritual life and need help because I'm just going through the motions and don't feel any real connection to God.

Once, you have identified this concerns, what can coaches do for you? They can:

1. Have conversations with you that you may not want to have. Often, you have unmet expectations or are falling short of your potential. Coaches see something in you that you don't see in yourself.

2. Challenge you to stretch and do things you may be unwilling to try. Capable coaches will defy you to think and respond in new ways you never imagined or believed you could.

3. Help you see and become something you couldn't visualize or become on your own. Even players who quit our team have become successful young women because the seeds of greatness were planted while they played and now the women have matured into their destiny. Sometimes a dream is planted but that destiny isn't fulfilled until later in life. Joseph in the Bible was given a dream at 17-years-old but had to complete 10 major tests before he could fulfill his destiny at age 30.

Ceilings were made to be broken through. Don't make the mistake of going a year without gaining new experiences, failing, and re-calibrating. Don't be satisfied with reaching the same ceiling year after year when you have so much room for upward mobility. Your talents were made to flourish, expand, and grow, not to stagnate.

The Two Secrets of the Coach and the Player: Separately They Never Make Magic

I bet at some point you have kept a secret. Whether it was something a friend told you or a surprise for your wife, you want to keep it close to your heart. Until you reveal it, it doesn't come to fruition. That's really the heart of the relationship with a coach. You have secret potential that has not emerged because you're not quite sure how to activate it. Your coach's secret is his ability to activate that latent potential that is dormant in your life. It's only when you bring your secret (your potential) and the coach's secret (the unique skill to unlock talent) together that the real magic happens.

> *My wife, Natalie, was a barrel of latent and undeveloped potential. She was working at a job that didn't use her true talents, as a sales rep for a company that sold Verizon phones and services. She had never been around anyone who challenged and pushed her to come out of her shell, and she was unaware of her true potential. She attended one workshop on my best-selling book* This Ain't No Practice Life *and in two hours her switch was flipped (and apparently mine was too as I was sweet on her). That book and those two hours began to awaken her imagination about what she could really do in the world, which was a lot. From that course she went on to start her own catering company, become a real pro at designing and decorating the properties, and began to manage all of our vacation rentals around the country. You see, she had a secret (her hidden potential) that she didn't really know that she had. I had a secret ability to open her eyes to her potential. When these two secrets came together, magic happened. It happened in more ways than one, as we went on to marry and have a daughter named Ella Grace. When I'm teaching people who have lots of potential but can't see it, I'm always reminded of the parable Jesus shared about sowing seed in the book of Matthew:*

>> "Once there was a man who went out to sow grain.[4] As he scattered the seed in the field, some of it fell along the path, and the birds came and ate it up.[5] Some of it fell on rocky ground, where there was little

soil. The seeds soon sprouted, because the soil wasn't deep. [6] But when the sun came up, it burned the young plants; and because the roots had not grown deep enough, the plants soon dried up.[7] Some of the seed fell among thorn bushes, which grew up and choked the plants.[8] But some seeds fell in good soil, and the plants bore grain: some had one hundred grains, others sixty, and others thirty."

Natalie came to that workshop with good soil. She was ready. For whatever reason, she had reached a place where she wanted more life, more passion, and more impact. Not everyone from that workshop went on to do great things. However, when her talent and passion was activated, I began to see her for what she could become, not what she had been. That potential was attractive to the world and me. She was ready to play at a whole new level.

I want you to think about what secret talent you've been hiding from the world that you want to let out. I want you to reflect on some uncertain part of your life. For many years, it was my faith and spiritual walk. I went to church but I was stagnant. I was restless. It wasn't until that restlessness grew strong enough that I decided to do something about it. We began to try out new churches looking for the spirit to touch and work in our hearts. In a Sunday morning service at New Vision Baptist, it came alive. *It was a game-changer.* It activated that hunger and spirit in us. While working on a new prospect one day for my business of coaching and training *the prospect* said to me, "You do realize what kind of platform you have been given to share your faith, don't you?" *My secret had been activated.* With my hunger and God-given abilities and that new pastor and church service, we now had a game to play in and win. The same thing happened with my physical health.

Two years ago, introduced by a mutual friend, I found my personal trainer Rod Key. I had been working out for years in secret but my workouts rarely if ever produced any significant results. Does this sound like you? I was just going through the motions and consistently hitting the ceiling. I was the same weight, and was disappointed, and then felt guilty that I wasn't putting in the work to get in the best shape of my life. I made the big decision to hire Rod and I began to work out at 5:00 a.m., followed by a daily devotion. This would provide a newfound energy to address both my confidence and my physical condition. Just as the new church activated my spiritual needs, Rod could challenge me in ways I couldn't challenge myself, and could help me dig deeper.

Don't you think it's time to let your secret out of the bag? Also, don't you believe it's time to find that ONE person who has the secret sauce on how to activate it? In his book *Eleven Rings*, Phil Jackson identifies his talent and says, "What I really do is transform disorganized teams into champions." He did it with the Chicago Bulls after coach Doug Collins couldn't and he did it with the Los Angeles Lakers when coach Dale Harris couldn't. Now, that secret is worth $12 million per year, whenever Jackson wants to coach. How much would your secret be worth if it was activated? You may never find out unless someone who has a trained eye can activate it and help you share it with the world.

A Good Coach Will Help You Go from a "Baby Star" to a "Big Star"

I live outside of Nashville, the country music capital of the world. The one thing I can always count on when flying out of the Nashville International Airport is seeing the many people who are walking through with no money, no clothes, and no clue of what their future holds. They have a guitar on their back and a dream in their heart and they have come to pursue that dream in Nashville. Some will remain "baby" stars and play off, off-Broadway for many years before giving up on their dreams. A few will make the critical transition from "baby star" to "big star" and will move from playing in front of 200 people in a tiny bar to playing before 20,000 fans at Nashville's Bridgestone Arena. They will go from making $200 in tips to earning more than $200,000 for the same show just a hundred yards away. I like to tell people that a good coach takes someone from being a "baby star" to becoming a "big star."

It doesn't happen randomly. While the strategies vary from coach to coach, I use a particular process. Here's what it might look like if I were coaching you.

We start with a **Dominant Aspiration**, which is a single tangible outcome you would like to drive in a one-year cycle as measured in 30-day windows. It could be a multiyear project but this ONE thing is the BIG thing. It is the championship you win or the gold medal you get—the one BIG thing that means the most to you.

We then eliminate all the white noise and get down to the highest value of your time spent TOWARD that dream. We call these activities "High-Value Activities" (thanks to business coach Mark Leblanc). We eliminate all the "Low-Value Activities," which are the things we do that have nothing to do with our dream and are not moving you closer to your dominant aspiration. Once we identify which of the activities has the highest value in relation to your dominant focus, we begin recalibrating your time around these daily activities.

We begin implementing a system, the vehicle that will carry you toward your aspiration. The distribution system is the means you need to achieve your big goals. It could be a marketing technique, a distribution channel, or a customer acquisition program. But you must have a system.

We then implement a scoreboard, because we have to know if you are winning and losing toward your big goal. I track two things: activity and results. You should work on at least three high-value activities every single day toward your big focus. (Now do you see why having the big focus is so critical to this equation?) With just three big wins per day toward your big goal you are building momentum, which is simply energy headed in a particular direction. Three big things per day multiplied times five days per week gets you to 15 big things every week toward the big focus. This is 60 specific activities per month and 720 per year. This is how you "accelerate" your path and what we should be measuring. Here's an illustration from the business world:

- My dominant focus for my company this year is $2.4 million in sales.
- Broken down, this is $200,000 of sales every 30 days.
- This is $600,000 per 90 days.

We measure our activity from our "selling and distribution system" every week to see what our high-value activities are in relation to our monthly goal. If we hit our goal 12 consecutive times (monthly), then it is likely that we will drive our ultimate focus of $2.4 million in revenue.

This is a quantitative focus. But what if you have a qualitative dominant aspiration? At one time in my life, I wrote on my white board at my home office that my ultimate aspiration was to become the next Stephen Covey. He had influenced my life so much and since he was getting older, I believed I could become the next generation Covey. This was my aspiration. Now, how would my system work?

I have an aspiration: Be the next Covey.

I decided what my high-value activities needed to be in order for me to become next Covey: Write impactful books, give powerful speeches all over the country, start my own podcast, go on tour, and continue to hone my craft, building momentum along the way.

I chose the "systems" I need to get my message out: Marketing and advertising, multiple profit centers around a core message, training the trainer, licensing, podcast, blogs, websites, speaking tours, DVDs, downloads, and our *Legacy Selling System* to attract speaking engagements and ultimately customers who turn into coaching assignments. I also scale our company much as Covey scaled Franklin Covey; the core message is distributed through multiple coaches, and products and services, including planners.

I track both our activity and results: Is our strategy working in a 30-day cycle? Are we hitting our monthly goals? Are we moving closer to the big focus weekly, monthly, and yearly?

Therefore, here's the question. How would we know if I became the next Stephen Covey or not? Would it be measured in book sales, number of people impacted, speaking engagements, size of our company became or brand recognition?

Do you see how hard it is to track and measure a qualitative aspiration versus a quantitative one? Although you may have big dreams (becoming a country music star), you need a quantitative tool (earning $100 million or selling 50 million albums) that can be tracked and measured.

Smart coaches build "mental models" and "processes" that break something very big into small steps. They help you course-correct and recalibrate. They look at your performance to see where you're missing something. They create the sequential processes necessary to reach your goals and prevent you from floundering.

Let's revisit the cowboy from Oklahoma who comes to Nashville who doesn't have a good coach and see what he does. First, he wastes lots of time and energy as an outsider trying to get on the inside. Instead of playing in front of the right people, he plays in front of all the wrong people in all the wrong places. He then lucks into playing in front of the right person one evening but he says all the wrong things. This cycle goes on for years (sometimes up to 10) as he "tries to figure it out on his own." Finally, 10 years later, he is too old to be a great country music star because the industry is trending downward in age; he has missed his window. He gets one chance and finally signs a publishing deal. But because he isn't business-savvy and doesn't have someone coaching him, he signs an unfavorable agreement. He earns very little and stays mad at "the establishment" for the rest of his life and goes to some obscure town where he plays weddings and parties for nominal fees.

Now, let's compare this to someone who has a coach who specializes in helping "baby stars" become "big stars." The aspirational music star comes to Nashville and connects with the right coach and mentor. That coach knows all the inside skinny on who's important and what clubs to play. From the beginning, the music star has the right vocal coaches, financial advisors, gigs, and the right course-correction. He performs in front of the real decision-makers, which speeds up his ability to sign a publishing deal or record contract. The coach helps him connect with the right talent developers who work on his look, vocals, stage presence, and more. These steps take three to five years versus 10. The right coach knows that most singers are commodities who have similar features, so he begins to differentiate him. The right coach knows the right marketing tools so the singer can build his fan base. This strategy works effectively because the coach has the insight and experience to guide the singer. This coach ACCELERATES the process and in year seven, the young "baby star" sells millions and millions of albums, becoming one of the hottest stars in the world, giving him financial security for his entire life. Credit the right coach!

A good coach accelerates the process. A good coach knows how to win. A good coach has a proven system of success. A good coach takes "baby stars" and turns them into "big stars."

The Prideful Resist a Good Coach

I firmly believe that everyone needs a coach but after coaching people for years and selling around the world, I've also learned that there are people simply don't "want" one. Initially, I would chase these people and try to convince them they needed me, *but not anymore.* I listen to them and I pursue them as clients or I cut bait after one conversation. I know in the first 15 seconds if you're ready to play at a new level or not. I won't chase you for months. I'm saying this for the benefit of these "lone wolves" as well the coaches dealing with them. People who say they don't need a coach have *pride*, deep-seated insecurity and fear just masked with pride. Pride, defined in the dictionary, is a feeling or deep pleasure or satisfaction derived from one's **own** achievements, the achievements of those with whom one is closely associated, or from qualities or possessions that are widely admired. There's a better definition: a feeling that you are more important or better than other people and have achieved every bit of your worldly success without the help of others. It sounds foolish when I put it that way, doesn't it? Pride is always the reason people say they don't want or don't need a coach. Moreover, no matter how capable the coach, it's very difficult to coach or develop someone who isn't receptive to the process. These people will consistently hit a ceiling but that's okay; they believe breaking through would just be too much work so they make excuses. Someone once told me, "My company will never allow me to have any more success than what I'm currently having so coaching wouldn't make sense for me." WOW. My response: You need to get a new company that wants and will allow you to have as much success as you can."

You'll spot a prideful, uncoachable client almost immediately when you hear comments such as:

- ▸ Well, my deal is somewhat unique and you probably wouldn't understand it.
- ▸ I'm already pretty good at what I do, and I don't believe I need a coach. What would you teach me? Or what do you know about my industry?
- ▸ I'm really the best in the world and have this under control.

Here is my counterargument:

- ▸ No one's deal is "unique"—it's only unique in your mind. Universal and timeless principles apply to every situation. You would be shocked how many people start off by saying, that their deal or market is unique. I always then whether they have to get customers. They say yes. I then say, "Well, it's not that unique, is it?" General principles of success are timeless and can be used in any industry to drive achievement.
- ▸ You may be "pretty good" at what you do but you're not as good as you could be. A complete stranger could walk

into your business or life and almost immediately notice areas in which you need improvement. Remember our saying, "You can't see the picture when you are inside the frame." You are too emotional about yourself so you can't be objective. This is why you can easily detect missing structures in others but cannot recognize your own shortcomings.

▶ You may actually be the best in the world at what you do (although it's highly unlikely). So what? Michael Jordan turned to trainer Tim Grover to coach him personally when played under Phil Jackson. Steve Jobs turned to management coach Bill Campbell. Jack Welch turned to global advisor Ram Charan. If some of the most accomplished people turn to coaches, why wouldn't you?

When I see people who are dead set against using a coach, they are:

▶ Stuck	▶ Unaware
▶ Apathetic	▶ Unenlightened
▶ Stubborn	▶ Stagnant
▶ Prideful	▶ Content

If you are one of these people, I know that *I can't help you.* You may even want to pass this book along to someone who you believe (there's that pride again) needs it. If you are selling to these people, unfortunately, you're in for a long miserable stretch trying to convince them they need you. If you are leading one of these people, at some point, you should expect him to destroy your team because of his selfish nature. Your constant frustration will lead to an enormous "emotional tax" on you and the team and become an "opportunity cost" because of the time and energy you will exert trying to get him on board and see what he doesn't want to see. My best advice for you would be to cut bait and run. In the future, don't allow the spirit of pride to affect you.

If you are hungry, humble, and coachable then proceed to chapter 2. I'll show you what a good coach can do to your life and how he or she can become a tremendous accelerator for your life.

Q & A WITH COACH BURT

Q: I don't know even where to start to find what I'm supposed to be doing and I'm not fulfilled. What can I do?

A: You can find your voice at the intersection of your talents (what you are naturally good at), your passion (what you love doing or are passionate about), what your conscience is prompting you to do (that still small voice nudging you toward action), and a need in the world that you can fulfill with your talent (think problem and you have the solution). I suggest you go to a quiet place and contemplate these hard questions. I suggest you talk with those closest to you and ask, "What do you think I'm really good at?" I also suggest you read the book *Unique Ability* by Catherine Nomura.

Q: I've hit a plateau in my life. I make the same amount of money, I'm bored with my work and life, and I'm in a rut. What can I do?

A: Plateaus are static states along with a gradual downward slide into complacency. When you hit a plateau, I suggest you raise your goals because they no longer excite you, probably because they're not big enough. They need to scare you; I went out and bought a million dollar house. See what that will do to motivate you out of complacency! You need to change your strategy in small steps to open up new doors. Working harder will not get you out of the plateau. You also need a hobby outside of work in which you can immerse yourself. Boredom is a function of doing the same thing with no change of scenery or challenges.

Q: I'm a baby star in the grand scheme of things but have a strong desire to become a big star in my field. What do I need to do to create this breakthrough?

A: This is a common problem for people who aspire to have a big impact in the world but feel stuck doing small stuff. Here is what I recommend you do to become a bigger star. 1) Find people who are already big stars and track their success path and timelines to see what they're doing that you can start implementing. 2) Find coaches who "know the game" that you don't know. Utilize experts who can take you and your brand to the big time. 3) Get better. You may not be a star because your skills are still at the junior level. 4) Improve your marketing and distribution. Some of the big stars aren't more talented but they know how to build a bigger audience and market their goods and services more effectively. I applaud you for having the right mindset. You should aim to be a big star and there are ways you can accelerate this journey.

2

FIND AND FILL YOUR MISSING STRUCTURES

When I met Tommy Davidson he was just a regular ole' real estate agent. He capped off at 45 deals per year, drank beer on the weekends, and generally just goofed off. He was a barrel of unrealized potential. I began to coach his real estate team in 2009 and I didn't believe for one minute that Tommy was paying any attention. He never took notes, he never really participated, and he never gave me any indication that he was on board with the team. *But he was.* He stared intently every time I gave a presentation and he asked for more coaching. He fixated on one concept I teach called "Person of Interest" in which you learn how to get attention for your brand and make the shift from a commodity to a recognizable brand. You become a "Person of Interest." From that training and subsequent sessions, Tommy decided that he would give himself a new name, "Good Time Tommy," complete with t-shirts, TV shows, podcasts, hats, shot glasses, big events, and more. The idea worked and he began to differentiate himself, although he was sometimes seen as controversial because many of his competitors didn't take the time or make the effort to understand his philosophy. This year, Tommy and his team are on track to complete 100 transactions; he has built an entire enterprise around these concepts becoming one of the most talked about agents in our market.

Before his successful rebranding, there was some structures missing from Tommy's efforts:

- ▸ He needed direction.
- ▸ He needed a plan.
- ▸ He needed a marketing play.
- ▸ He needed a brand.
- ▸ He needed a team.
- ▸ He needed confidence to do things differently from all the other agents.

In short, he needed a coach.

Once he had all these things, he was on his way.

A missing structure is a void. It's a hole. It's a gap that if you filled, you could literally be sitting on "Acres of Diamonds." But if you can't see that void, you can't fill it. That's where a coach comes in. A good one will find and fill these gaps in your work and personal life. There's an old saying, "Money only changes hands when problems are solved." You have a problem and someone could help you solve it. However, if you reach out to that person, you are admitting your vulnerability and lack of confidence.

All I can say is get over yourself!

In my book *Person of Interest* I said that there were seven core ingredients shared by the "people of interest." Take a look at these seven factors and see if you're coming up short in any of them.

The Seven Traits Shared by People of Interest

1. **Knowledge**—You don't have enough specific knowledge in a concentrated area to create a breakthrough. You are not considered an expert or you are an expert but not enough people in your market know it. You are still a "secret agent."

2. **Skill**—Your delivery of that knowledge doesn't turn people on and in fact, may turn people off. Skill is the ability to take knowledge and share it in a way that resonates with other people. You may know something but still be unable to sell it.

3. **Effort**—You will not do the inconvenient work that you need to be successful. This is where desire and passion come in. You may have the knowledge and even the skill but if you're not willing to do whatever it takes, you will not be able to re-calibrate.

4. **Confidence**—You have an insecurity, which prevents you from advancing. You achieve some success but can't master new responsibilities. Confident people seek risk and opportunity. Insecure people want comfort and complacency.

5. **Likability**—Your energy is low, you may appear selfish, or your personality is not very strong. Consequently, instead of attracting people, you are repelling them. Likable people are open, inviting, and humble. People who are not likable seem disconnected and are not seen as friendly.

6. **Connectivity**—You struggle to connect to different kinds of people. As a result, you only interact with like-minded

people and therefore cannot grow your networks and expand. Stepping into new arenas means possible rejection, not acceptance; your self-confidence can't take that step so you just play it safe.

7. **Deep Networks**—You have small and shallow networks and not enough people fighting for you or providing support. You only build effective networks when you are willing to get lost in their dreams, create unique value for those in that network, and build others up. We call this advocacy.

Shortcomings in these seven areas are the most common missing structures I see. Without a coach telling you that your networks are too small or your likability factor is low, you will just continue to hit the repeat button but never really move ahead. On the other hand, if you filled any or all of these missing structures, you could really move ahead. Some of you won't be interested in "fixing" them but those of you who are willing are headed for success.

Every business model, including mine, has missing structures in it that are easy for outsiders to identify. Our approach of finding and filling missing structures is a much less offensive method than saying, "You have five big problems." This methodology works for any type of business that has gaps.

Most likely, you're too close to your work so you cannot see what structures are missing in your work. That is why you need a skilled expert who can help you recognize and then work through the gaps in your business. There are a variety of situations in which you may need help such as:

- Direction about what to do with a failing employee.
- Confidence to stop procrastinating and take action toward a new direction or vision.
- The need to hear an outsider say your perception of the market isn't accurate.
- New strategies on how to start and grow the business.
- "Professional accountability" because you know you have the potential to play at a higher level but need some tough love and guidance to set up the right strategy.

Ten Typical Missing Business Structures

1. A pure selling system to acquire new customers in a consistent and systematic manner.

2. A clear marketing plan of how you will reach your target audience.

3. A **Person of Interest** Strategy on how to become the go-to person in your market and increase your perceived value so you become well known and a "hot asset."

4. A developed and packaged strategy highlighting what makes you "look different and run faster" than your competitors.

5. An onboarding system or training plan for new hires, intermediate, or top performers so they to continue to develop. This system is rarely found in small businesses which is why their employees often fail to progress. (Our Talent Supply program addresses this on the sales side with the 90-Day Sales manager concept. See more at www.thetalentsupply.com.)

6. A recruiting system to hire new and better performers for your team. To be effective at recruiting you need a philosophy about who you want and why, an available talent pool, and a world-class sales pitch to persuade people to come over to your team.

7. A retention system to keep top talent from wanting to leave for better opportunities. (More on this in the next chapter when I explain the "Whole Person Theory" and how to value the body, mind, heart, and spirit.)

8. A weekly meeting aimed at keeping your team spending their highest value time on the dominant focus. This meeting involves accountability and scoring mechanisms along with checkpoints and coaching.

9. A dominant focus or tangible outcome you would like to drive in a 12-month cycle as measured in 30-day windows. You need a specific target and not just say you want to do better this year than last.

10. A plan to scale your business so that is operates like a well-oiled machine independently of you while providing you with a monthly revenue stream.

We all have "missing structures." The faster we learn to find and fill them the sooner we start solving bigger problems, which leads to more profits. One of the most common missing structures is accountability. While a coach can help you be accountable by staying focused and eliminating the clutter, there are actually two types of accountability. Let me explain the difference between "amateur accountability" and "professional accountability."

Amateur accountability is needed because you lack any sense of discipline. You won't get out of bed, you won't make your phone calls, you won't go the distance, and you won't do any of the basics that you need to do to win in the market. I like to tell people, "You can go to the gym on your own the workouts you do by yourself are basically nonexistent." When you hire a trainer, your workouts are real workouts with real sweat and real calories burned.

Professional accountability is when you know deep inside that you need a professional to help you navigate through a new rite of passage. The coach will support, direct, counsel, and propel. He or she will show you new improved strategies that you didn't know. The coach will challenge your current status, pushing you beyond your comfort zones. The coach will force you to "take it to the limit."

Obviously, I wish everyone wanted "professional account-ability." The great coach Mike Krzyzewski at Duke used to say, "If you come in below where you need to be I'll spend all of my time trying to get you where you should have been to begin with. If you come in where you should be every day, I'll spend my time taking you to a new level you never even imagined."

Take a break now and think about what your "missing struc-tures" are. Are you an amateur or a professional? It is okay to admit that you are an amateur and that you need help, but don't buy your own hype and believe that you are so good that you don't at need a professional to help you elevate to the next level.

Finding Your KRYPTONITE, the One Thing that Consistently Holds You Back

When I made the decision to position myself as **The Super Coach** a colleague of mine said, "Superman had kryptonite, and maybe one thing you do is help people find theirs." In the movies, Lex Luthor used Superman's kryptonite to neutralize his super powers. The reality is that we all have some kryptonite, one weakness that is holding us back. If we eliminated it, there is no limit to what we could accomplish. Superior coaches don't have a "one-size-fits-all" approach because they know that your Achilles heel isn't the same as someone else's. Nevertheless, in business, employees at all levels usually have one or more fatal flaws that prevent them from activating their potential. One significant problem is not having a world-class "explanation of services" (EOS). This places them squarely in a commodity trap of saying the same thing everybody else says. We've been taught to sell features and benefits. Simon Sinek, the author of *Start with Why* said, "People don't buy what you do; they buy why you do it." My good friend and top producer Tom Love combined Sinek's theory with my work in *Person of Interest* to create a world-class formula for explaining your services. It can be a game changer so we have adopted this philosophy and now teach it to others in our coaching programs.

A good EOS has six parts that include:

1. First, tell me what you believe versus what you don't. People don't buy what you do; they buy why you do it. (For more about this concept, read See Simon Sinek's book.) When you lead with what you believe in and the other person believes you in the first 15 seconds, keep going. If the other person doesn't believe you, cut bait and run.

2. Then tell me why you believe what you believe, to see if I believe it too. I don't know about you but I do business and vote for politicians who share my beliefs. If you do this the right way, the 15-second rule also applies and the other person's body language will tell you everything you need to know.

3. Pivot and tell me what you "really do" versus your title. For example, a nurse may say, "I'm a nurse." With some coaching she could say, "I wake up to save people's lives." The latter statement is much more compelling and gets the nurse out of the commodity trap. Reduce your job description into simple words so people clearly know what you can actually do for them when they enter into a relationship with you.

4. Tell me three ways you do it differently from others. We discussed this step in our book, *Zebras & Cheetahs: Look Different and Stay Agile to Survive the Business Jungle* Explain how your services differ from those available elsewhere. You have to make these distinctions very clear so connect the dots.

5. Provide "social proof" of other clients and the results you have achieved in a field similar to the one in which you're pitching. In the science of persuasion, this is called "consensus" and helps to build your credibility with the prospect.

6. Finally, ask the million-dollar question, "If I could do this for you just as I've done it for all of these other people, then what would prohibit us from doing business with each other?" What good is explaining what you do if you can't ask someone if you could do it for them?

It is essential you take the time to work through this EOS, which drives your position in the market, who you recruit, the customers you seek, how you market and brand your services, and every other facet of your business. When you're doing business with people who don't believe the same things you do or

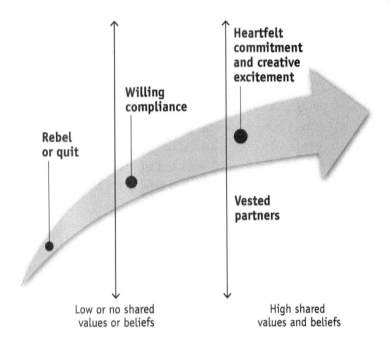

don't value what you do, then you end up with misaligned values and customers who take all the life and energy out of you and your team. On the other hand, having shared values will increase the commitment levels of your customers.

When we "believe" the same things, we build a "vested partnership." This is when I advocate and fight for you in the market and you advocate and fight for me. When we don't believe the same things, I give you very minimal effort and I may even rebel or quit. I become a detractor of yours in the market or on my best day, a passive partner. All of this is transactional and not transformational. Willing compliance is a very low form of commitment to each other. It's more like obligation. If you give the EOS correctly, you should know in the first 15 seconds if you have a potential partner or not, which saves you the headache of chasing someone for 15 months. Your close ratios, which represent the number of people with whom you share your explanation of services who ultimately buy your products, will go through the roof because others will see you as having a "special sauce" that is unique, differentiated, and interesting. Remember, the opposite of interesting is boring. (See my book *Person of Interest*.)

Another major problem for business professionals is that they don't have a "selling system" and they don't prospect near enough. They have no specific game plan on how to acquire customers. The purpose of any business is to create a customer so nothing is more important than spending time with your current customers or trying to get new ones. A selling system is like a game plan in coaching. Can a coach who only has three plays that don't work win many games? Of course not.

This was my problem when I left athletic coaching and became an entrepreneur. I didn't have a game plan. I didn't have an EOS. I didn't know my real value. I didn't have a model to be accountable to every single day. I quickly figured out that we were not generating enough leads (new business) because we didn't have enough strategies. In the sports world we went into every single game with a play sheet. We developed one after studying the market and competition (by watching video of other teams' games) and we cultivated a "game plan" to win. We would go right down the play sheet in the game and chart to see what worked and what didn't. At halftime, I would recalibrate to use only the plays that worked and we would run them until somebody stopped them. If the plays were working, we never changed them. On the other hand, most salespeople (or anyone for that matter) keep running their plays even when they're not working. Again, the salesperson may not be able to see or admit that the way he has always done things is no longer generating sales or new business. If you are not hitting your sales goals, chances are you're not getting enough opportunities, most likely because you are not using enough strategies.

In our selling system, we use a number of tactics to drive leads including:

1. **Hit List**—These are 10 people we are going after each week to get their attention and share our "explanation of services." We believe these people fit in a pre-determined filter of individuals we would like to serve with our product or service. For managers or coaches these could be your recruits or targets. The hit list represents any potential new revenue or opportunity.

2. **Farm Club**—These are five "high value targets" with whom we are going to go for the close. We use the recommended seven to 15 touches in the follow up, using a challenger style when we follow up to create movement. (The challenger style comes from the book *The Challenger Sale* by Adamson and Adamson. This style pushes the prospect by stressing the value of how you can solve the prospect's problem better than the competition.) The prospect will allow you to "challenge him" because you are an expert who teaches, trains, and tailors content to fit his needs. You are always two steps ahead of him with your thought processes and solutions.

3. **Net Promoters**—Our strategy is to quickly turn a new customer into a promoter and ultimately into an advocate. This happens when you exceed the customer's expectations and provide added "freebies." The minute we obtain new customers our goal is to create real value for them that they can't get anywhere else.

4. **Top 25**—We believe that 25 deep and meaningful relationships in the market could make you millions and millions of dollars per year. This comes by maintaining constant engagement and top-of-mind value to these 25 people over and over. Each week we try to touch three of our top 25 in a positive and meaningful manner. With the Top 25 strategy, we seek to cultivate 25 people who know us, love us, and will provide referrals. We treat these people like VIP's and we are always there for them both personally and professionally. Because of this unique partnership, these people become "multipliers" for our business and feed us new business.

5. **Connectors**—We believe in the concept of "six degrees of separation" and know that through the proper connections we can get access to virtually anyone in the world. We identify two connectors per week who have influence and use our relationship with them to connect us to top decision-makers. The connector strategy makes these introductions "warm" vs. "cold."

6. **Climbers**—The world is full of up and coming talent. We identify these climbers and embed ourselves with these future leaders. Climbers could be future customers who can't afford to buy today but will someday, or they could be potential future employees. We identify two climbers per week.

7. **The Showcase**—A showcase is a strategy in which you bring your key players, potential clients, and past clients together to harness their energy and spotlight your power. You could hold an educational event, entertainment outing or a combination of the two. We

aim to have one event each month and four major ones annually.

8. **The Database**—We have roughly 10,000 people in our database, which is growing daily. I send out weekly messages that have an open ratio of 18% to 21%, which comes because I personally write all of my content. (The open ratio represents the percentage of people who actually open the e-mail indicating interest. Most database strategies only have an open ratio of 8% to 10%.) The database creates a call to action, keeps you top-of-mind, and offers your followers something valuable. Too many people drastically underestimate the value of this database or send out junk, which is why they rarely build a following.

9. **The Free Prize**—This is about constantly creating some "unique value" for your customers that they never expect. (I discuss this in detail in *Person of Interest*.) This is the plus one and the icing. You are being compensated for one reason: to get results. However, if you get those results and then some, you become a must-have versus a nice to have. The "free prize" is a tangible or intangible, meaning something of value that we cannot measure such as trust, chemistry, energy, focus, likability or drive, in addition to the transaction that the consumer never expected. It can be a tiebreaker if you face competition for this customer.

These are just nine of the strategies we use every single week to drive our business. I haven't even discussed social media and other tactics. The message here is that you need a range of strategies and shouldn't rely on one or two. Most salespeople cling to purchasing leads, relying too heavily on referrals, or light networking. In today's saturated and competitive world, that is just not enough. (In my next book, I'll be describing even more strategies as part of our Legacy Selling System.)

The third shortcoming most business professionals share is a lack of "follow-up." Salespeople operate from a temporary mind-set. It would be nice if we could close every client in one call on the first attempt but this rarely happens. Studies show that 80% of the time, it takes seven to 15 touches to convert a suspect to a prospect but many people never go that far. They stop after touch one or two. Not only is it vital to go back to those who have indicated interest but also to go back in the right way. There are several key principles you should use when you're trying to move someone off the fence during the sales process:

1. If you understand the laws of attraction, you understand that a person can be attracted to something in the morning and completely forget about it in the afternoon. This is called "object impermanence." Think about when children are completely focused on one toy but when they turn their head and you remove it, they forgot it was even there. Prospects move on quickly to things that are not there which is why you must constantly touch them and stay in their lives.

2. We never call a prospect back and say, "I was just thinking of you," or "You were on my mind this morning." When we go back to a customer, we use a challenger mind-set to do one thing: make them think. Relationship builders want to resonate. Challengers want to reframe. I want my prospects to get off the phone with me and go, "WOW, no one I've spoken to gave me that

kind of value. He challenged me." The world is full of relationship builders who supplicate to the prospect. Are you an expert or not? Do you know what you are doing or not? If you do, stop putting yourself in an inferior position; start putting yourself in an elevated position because of your knowledge, your skills, your desire, and your confidence.

3. Remember, the goal of any follow-up is to articulate how your skills can solve the client's problem better than anyone else can and to create action. All other touches are just FLUFF.

4. When we reach touch #7 we ask the real question, "Have you noticed how hard we have worked to earn your business?" They typically say "yes." We then ask, "Then what is stopping us from doing business with each other? We believe the same things. We brought you exactly what you have been looking for and we are ready to create unique value for you."

Different Types of Customers

We believe there are four types of customers. (This approach is based partly on the work of Fred Reichheld of *The Ultimate Question*):

1. **Passives**—These are customers who are lukewarm toward you and your services.
2. **Detractors**—These are customers who have done business with you but are dissatisfied and are hurting your perceived value in the market.
3. **Promoters**—These are customers who are pleased with your business and will make some chatter to others.

4. **Advocates**—These are people who are way beyond pleased with your services because you have exceeded their expectations and they are "fighting for you in the market." This is where all of your new business comes from in the form of referrals.

The Road to Hell Is Paved with Good Intentions

In one of the best-selling books of all time, *The Purpose Driven Life: What on Earth Am I Here For?*, by Pastor Rick Warren, I found the perfect description of accountability. Pastor Warren said we need accountability to help us break through a common vicious cycle:

- ▶ We all start with good intentions.
- ▶ We fail to act or follow through.
- ▶ We experience ensuing guilt.

I am elaborating on Pastor Warren's words. The word "accountability" means to be accountable to something or someone. Many see that someone as their coach who holds them accountable to a system or structure that could produce a new outcome in their life. With accountability and consequences, we can shift our behavior and do what is necessary to cultivate the important habits of success.

Let us start with good intentions. It is thought that Saint Bernard of Clairvaux created the saying, "The road to hell is paved with good intentions." We all start with good intentions. We want to eat better, live longer, make our sales calls, spend more time with our families, take more vacations, spend more time in the church, volunteer more, go to the doctor and dentist, and become what we envision. We intend to, but never do. In an incredibly powerful book, *The Power of Intention*, author

Wayne Dyer spoke of planting the seeds of your future into the universe and the universe lining up with those intentions. Too many people do not have any intentions or only very small ones. If you believe that money only changes hands when problems are solved, then you must start with this intention, "I want to find and solve major problems in the world." For example, many companies are investing in "driverless cars." You will simply get in, state your destination you and then spend your time relaxing or working. What problems does this intention solve? There are an estimated 55,000 deaths per year from human error in automobile accidents, and thousands of hours of lost productivity due to traffic. These cars solve both of these problems. Waking up to save human lives is a good intention to have.

My book *Small Towns Big Dreams* was aimed at showing how residents of small towns could accomplish big things in their world. In the book I said, "Every action we take is driven by our thoughts and our thoughts are no wiser than our understandings" (which I borrowed from *The Richest Man in Babylon*). In essence, if we have small intentions (thoughts), we wake up and take small actions, and small actions solve small problems and receive small rewards. You need GIGANTIC intentions. You need LARGE actions to get LARGE returns. Good intentions rarely are acted on unless the intention is so powerful that it gets your passion level up. You need something that gets you out of bed, something that keeps you up at night, and something that you can't quit talking about. You need a BIG INTENTION tied to your big purpose.

You may start with good intentions but then have another problem—you just can't follow through. My friend Matt Manero, author of *The Grit*, always says, "Momma lied when she told you the first step was the hardest. It's actually steps two, three, and four that are the hardest." One definition I frequently use for motivation is "taking an idea (intention) and seeing it through to its logical conclusion." That means you have the discipline (a derivative of the word disciple) to start, recalibrate, fight through adversity, and FINISH. This is where most people fall off the wagon. Consider the following scenarios:

- ▶ Have you ever started a new diet only to revert to your old way of eating?
- ▶ Have you ever made a promise to get your workout in first thing in the morning only to not work out at all?
- ▶ Have you made a commitment to go to church only to choose to watch football game instead?
- ▶ Have you made a commitment to make your prospecting calls only to goof off?
- ▶ Have you made a commitment to budget and save money only to buy something WAY over your budget?
- ▶ Have you ever promised that you would work a system "religiously" only to go back to the way you've already done it?

Remember new results require new behavior. Every new stimulus requires a new response. What got you here cannot get you there. Again, I use my own life as an example of using a coach to ensure I follow through. When I'm home, I use a personal trainer who I see at 6:00 a.m. This requires me to wake up at 5:15 a.m. to be in the gym at 6. He works me incredibly hard and I sometimes want to quit but he won't let me. He holds me accountable and pushes me. I am sure you can think of examples from your work life where accountability has made all the difference. It's why sales meetings are critical, weekly key performance indicators are vital, daily coaching sessions are necessary, and results have to be made transparent. Unfortunately, there are several reasons why so many people find follow through difficult:

1. Lack of overall discipline—Discipline, as stated, is a derivative of the word disciple, which means give yourself to a person or cause you believe in. People usually say they believe in their own future but they can't answer the question, "Where does your future reside?" I say, "It resides in your own imagination; therefore, you are the only person who can see it." You need to become a disciple to that future and have the "self-discipline" to create that future. Jesus had 12 disciples who all "followed him" to his logical conclusion to the crucifixion (Except for Judas who betrayed him). Discipline is the ability to follow a plan and see it all the way through to the end.

2. Too many priorities/conflicting priorities—Many people have too many activities and interests which dilute their time, energy, resources, and creativity. They need someone to help cut through the clutter so they can get clarity about their bigger future and what actions most align with what they want to accomplish.

3. Laziness—It's so much easier to take the path of least resistance. Remember that only unsatisfied needs motivate not satisfied needs. Even big producers get complacent because things get easy or they want to check out emotionally. A good coach can motivate, inspire and offer ways to be engaged. A good coach can awaken your faculties and passions if they've been dormant and you've been on autopilot.

The Power of a System

When we have a system, just look what can happen:
In September 1961, an overweight woman from Queens, New York, called a group of friends over to her house and confessed that eating cookies was her obsession. Her name was Jean Nidetch, and with that first admission, she discovered that one of the most effective keys to weight control is "empathy, rapport and mutual understanding." Her discovery resulted in a 70-pound weight loss and one of the most successful weight-control organizations in the world—Weight Watchers.

4. Lack of clarity about what action to take—You may not follow though because you just don't know what to do. You don't have a plan or system so you just drift into never-never land. (This is a big problem particularly for managers who haven't properly trained their staff. If you have this problem, consider our Legacy Selling System.)

Without accountability, there is a vicious cycle of good intentions followed by a lack of follow-through? Then guilt ensues.

1. We know we have missed a tremendous opportunity.
2. We know we have made and broken a promise to ourselves.
3. We know there will be consequences to our behavior that could affect our future.
4. Deep down we know we are better than what we are showing or producing.
5. We know what our problem is (like overeating) but we can't seem to control it on our own.

Many years ago, I had a player who had little or no self-discipline. She had coasted through much of her life on pure ability only to find out that others had superior abilities when she got to a higher level. She fought me every day as I tried to stretch her and hold her accountable. She ultimately quit our team saying that I didn't like her and wouldn't give her a fair chance. It was actually the opposite. I liked her and saw her tremendous potential but noticed her lack of follow-through and the guilt she always experienced when she didn't perform. After she quit I lost touch with her for almost 15 years until I received this message:

Hi, Coach! How are you? Congratulations on your engagement! I just wanted to thank you for the time you invested in me. All of the principles you instilled in us still sticks with me today. One thing that stuck with me most was looking someone in their eye when you're talking to them or when they're talking to you! I remember when I'd talk to you, I would look everywhere but your eyes and you'd follow me like a hawk! Haha, but, now, I do this. Sometimes, without even knowing! I have the book you read to us STILL plus a military version. You have played a part, SUBSTANTIALLY, in the woman I've become. You weren't just our basketball coach, you were our life coach. I catch myself implementing your lessons in my day-to-day life. I am so VERY thankful for you. My parents are, also. My father often says, "Val had a coach that wouldn't let her stray. We need coaches like that today." I just wanted to take time and thank you. God bless you, Coach.

A good coach will provide an accountability structure; he or she should make you write out plans for how you will execute your dominant goal and hold you accountable to your vision. If you don't have a vision, the coach will help you devise one. Ideally, a coach can work with you to shrink the gap between what you want to do and what you are doing at the present. The coach will push and prod to stretch you to failure when you want to give up prematurely.

You must first eliminate regret by taking action and building a high internal trust reserve with yourself so you know that you can make and keep commitments to yourself first. Private victories always precede public victories. You must first win the internal battle before you win the external battle.

The Missing Structure of a Time System

The phrase "time management" is a buzzword in business but in fact, time management is a myth. No one can speed up, slow down, or stop time. All we can do is prioritize what we plan to do with it. We can start every week with a clear plan on how we attack. That's what I've done as an athletic coach and a business coach. I would study our competitors for hours and then carefully put together the best strategies I thought would yield the biggest return for our team. I studied where I could exploit the competitors' weaknesses and where I thought they would exploit our weaknesses I sought to become a cheetah versus a turtle. I believe those who prepare and plan dramatically outperform those who don't any day of the week. However, when I started coaching in the business arena, almost no one had a strategy on how they would win. In essence, they were playing defense versus offense.

We all have 24 hours in a day, 86,400 seconds, and 168 hours in a week. **The top performers know they only get paid when**

they create results. Bureaucrats get paid by the hour or by the day, not necessarily on the results they achieve. Coaches get paid more when they produce more wins. How we view time and how we attack the "highest use of that time" is critical toward driving the results that pay us the most, whether in *love, money, recognition, reputational capital, and affirmation.*

I very much believe what Dan Sullivan, founder of Strategic Coach®, teaches what he refers to as an Entrepreneurial Time System®. I use his system, which is based on the following:

- ▶ We all choose how we utilize each of the 365 days in a year.
- ▶ There are three types of days in this system: Free, Focus, and Buffer.
- ▶ **Free days** are a period of 24 hours of complete freedom "away" from your business. This is for your rejuvenation and high achievers will find this their hardest day.
- ▶ **Focus days** are "money-generating" days where 80% of your time should be spent on activities that generate profits. In this book, I've explained our money-generating activities or what we call "High-Value Activity," which is tied to our Legacy Selling System (a comprehensive and coordinated attack on the market to generate exposure, leads, and new business). Be aware of low and high value ways you spend your time.
- ▶ **Buffer days** are "back stage" days when you can catch up, plan, strategize, and improve your processes and systems.

Like many entrepreneurs, you are probably stressed because of the constant pressure to produce. Between this stress and the volume of work, you may be on autopilot. That's why using the system of Focus, Buffer and Free days can be so effective. I tell my clients to think of these days as if they're athletes on a team:

- ▶ Free days are "off days" when you let your mind out to play, you are free to relax and enjoy all that life has to offer. These days are good for the soul and open you up to explore new ideas and expand your mind.
- ▶ Focus days are "game days" when you need to be completely focused on one thing, performing at very high levels of production with value creation for those who are paying to see you perform. These are your client-focused days or prospecting days.
- ▶ Buffer days are "practice days" when you are honing your craft and improving your talents. These are back-stage days that I call "comfortable days" because I typically wear relaxed clothes to the office or work from my home office, or even out of the office at a creative space.

Think of yourself as an athlete or entertainer. You only do three things: **You rest, you practice, and you perform.** No entertainer can ever perform for 365 days per year without burning out. Only when you can consistently replenish the body, mind, heart, and spirit are you rejuvenated.

Dan Sullivan's system is hard for people understand at first. Many people, including me, fight it, thinking that we can never take that many days off and still make money. Sullivan is known for only working 200 days per year (either Focus or Buffer days) and the remaining days off to do whatever he wants. In addition, he runs a $20 million-plus company!

I didn't think this was possible until I saw it with my own eyes through his coaching program and when I traveled to Florida to spend time with top lifestyle entrepreneur Scott Nagy. I arrived at Scott's $1.7 million home on a weekday to see him sitting perched up on his carriage house smoking a cigar. His new strategy was to take two years off and reassess his situation after he had sold his real estate company at the age of 41 for millions of dollars. He then moved to Seaside, Florida, on the coast of the state's panhandle, one of the hottest vacation destinations in the world, and purchased a short-term rental property. When I asked him how much his short-term rentals earned per year, he said, "Six figures in year one." I then asked him what he did every day at his job. He said, "Play golf, manage my properties, take my Bronco out for a ride, and eat breakfast, lunch, and dinner at the Cowgirl Kitchen nearby." Now, I want some of that, don't you?

We've been trained to burn the candle at both ends and work ourselves into a frenzy and then say we deserve a vacation. However, Sullivan and Nagy are actually saying that work should serve our life, not run our lives.

A good coach helps you gain perspective on:

- ▸ Why you need both entrepreneurial and coaching skills to win in today's competitive climate
- ▸ A system of looking at time in a new way that helps you control it versus it controlling you
- ▸ A new way of looking at yourself as an athlete or an entertainer who does three things: rest, practice, and play.

How to Lose All Your Confidence and Get it All Back

Early in my coaching career, I wrote down on a piece of paper, "A player who has confidence can do almost anything. A player without confidence can do nothing." This revelation when I was a high school coach would later in life prompt me to write the book *SWAG: 6 Battle Tested Strategies to Build and Protect Your Confidence*. Little did I know that many years later I would see exactly how much a liability confidence could become for the person who doesn't have any. At age 25 and just starting to win a lot of games in my coaching career (we were 28-3 in that breakout year) I fell in love. When I say in love, I mean stark raving crazy in love. Blind love. Over the top love. Ridiculous love. I just knew this woman was the one God had sent me to marry. The only problem I had was that she didn't share that belief. In a lunch meeting almost a year into our relationship in my hometown and with an engagement ring in my pocket she said to me, "I love you, Micheal. I just don't love you enough to marry you." I countered with something only a person who had given up every bit of his confidence to another would say: "How much do you have to love someone to marry them because I know married couples that don't love each other that much." I was lost. I was weak and I was wounded. For more than six months, I was in a deep depression. I was sick every single morning because in my distressed and weakened weak state I actually believed I had created this mess. I had no confidence and I needed to get it back fast because I was the head coach of a vibrant and growing program and my team desperately needed me.

During that period, one of my best friends, Tavi Fontana, a woman about 10 years older than me, shared one of the most revealing things I've ever heard about confidence and rejection that I would later use many times in my coaching career. She said, "Micheal, the way you are looking at this is all wrong. There is no such thing as rejection. She may not want what you have to offer but lots of people, including me, will." Here I was getting attention from one of the most beautiful women around and I couldn't even see it because I was so focused on the past. I have come to see this period of depression, which included me taking medication to bounce back, as one of the most pivotal moments of my life. Tavi became my relationship coach who affirmed and validated my worth and potential so clearly that I eventually begin to see it in my own self. From that point on I made a vow that I would protect my confidence and NEVER allow an outside circumstance or another person to take away what was mine. Tavi showed me the truth—many people will reject what you have but many people will want exactly what you've got. From this experience I begin to say, "Some will buy what you are selling, some won't buy what you are selling, so what? Just keep on moving."

The importance of self-confidence can't be underestimated and it is a vital focus of both personal and business coaches. Here are key points:

1. Confidence is essential to your success. Without it, you always revert to old habits and complacency. Confident people want risk and opportunity. Insecure people want to go where they feel safe and will not be rejected.
2. Confidence built up over years can be torn down in mere seconds. If we are not careful and we don't have a good coach, we become susceptible to believing what

other people say, which can destroy our confidence. When nobody believed in Rocky Balboa, his coach did and that belief propelled him into believing in himself. We all need that one person who sees our unlimited potential.

3. A specific strategy will help you build, maintain, and protect your asset of confidence and won't allow it to become a liability. With trained eyes, good coaches can detect when you are low on SWAG and offer you a refill, akin to refilling your car's tank when it is low on gas.

Abraham Maslow, the father of self-actualization, said "self-actualized" people who had reached their deepest potential shared 16 traits. He believed a self-actualized person could become totally independent of the good opinion of others and his confidence won't be dependent on what other people think about them. This concept is vitally important for people who are aiming to do big things since they will inevitably attract attention, criticism, detractors, and even extreme opposition.

Many years ago, the director of mental training for the St. Louis Cardinals came on my radio show to discuss his philosophy. The Cardinals had just come off back-to-back World Series wins, so he and the team were obviously doing something that worked. I asked him, "Is there anyone on the team who you have to really push to get confidence training?" He said, "Sure, the ones who are sitting on the bench or are about to be sent back down to the minor leagues." The big-time players had weekly sessions with him to work on their greatest asset—their confidence. The weaker players didn't think this training was important.

Think of your confidence in this way:

1. Confidence typically follows knowledge, skills, and desire.
2. When you are low on either knowledge or skills your confidence will suffer.
3. You can generate desire and "fake it" but with few skills or little knowledge you know deep down you have not paid the price to be good so your confidence can take a hit.

A whole person builds confidence by working on the four parts of his or her nature in a consistent and systematic manner.

If you are trying to build and protect this asset of confidence, do this:

1. *For the body*—Get in physical shape and work on skill development. To do this, I always recommend hiring a personal trainer.
2. *For the mind*—Constantly engage in learning and trying new things. Constantly change and improve to avoid boredom.

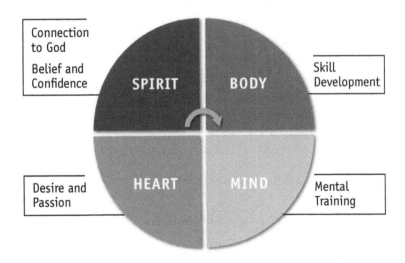

3. *For the heart*—Place yourself in your strength zone, your intuitive and instinctual area of performance that plays to your assets. (See and take The Kolbe Index, created by Kathy Kolbe, at www.kolbe.com.)

4. *For the spirit*—Connect with God on a consistent basis. Believe in yourself and the vision of where you and your company could go.

If one or more of these parts of nature are not being engaged, a person will begin to check out, either emotionally, physically, or spiritually. To win at the highest level you need to commit all four parts of your nature. Years ago, I explained that teams lose because of a lack of commitment of the heart, mind or spirit. At the time, people thought I was crazy because many coaches couldn't understand how these four parts are tied to confidence and execution. Think of it this way:

▸ If I lose faith in you then it affects my confidence (the spirit).

▸ If I get my heart broken by you then it affects my confidence (the heart).

▸ If I am bored with you then it affects my confidence (the mind).

▸ If I never get any better at my skills then I ultimately lose my confidence because I become obsolete in the world (the body).

A good coach comes into your life and FEEDS all of these parts:

1. You teach me skills and help me develop discipline for my body.

2. You constantly engage me so I am learning new strategies and growing my mind.

3. You validate my heart with recognition and opportunities to play in my unique ability zone.
4. You feed my spirit by helping me envision a bigger future and connect to God in more meaningful ways.

By now, I hope you see there is more than meets the eye when it comes to protecting your self-confidence. I always like to remember what the great coach Lou Holtz once said, "What takes years to build up can take seconds to tear down."

It's TIME You Empty Out Your "Hurt Pocket"

For years, I've fought the concept that I was a "life coach" for many but I have since come to accept that title. After all, you cannot talk about the whole person and the heart and spirit without tending to an integrated life. Pastor Jimmy Evans once delivered a sermon on the "Hurt Pocket," a tiny pocket of the heart where you store all of your pain from the past. While I coached one of my best friends through a breakup, I was reminded of how my past hurt affected my future. I was reminded of how difficult it was just to make it through an hour at a time, amid feelings of loss and hopelessness. Until we empty out our hurt pocket, we will continue to make all our future relationships pay for what happened to us in the past. This will happen in both our professional and personal lives. We must always make our future bigger than our past. To do this we must understand some key principles:

1. There is no such thing as rejection. People simply want something other than what we have to offer, but many people *will* want what we have.
2. Our past becomes the raw material for our bigger future. Whatever hell you are experiencing right now will give you the education you'll need later.

3. All the mistakes we made in our past are really just "market testing" for the future.

4. Until we empty out the hurt pocket, we will carry our emotional baggage into every encounter, which will sabotage our potential.

One night while listening to Wayne Dyer speak, I forgave my father for being absent early in my life. I've since come to believe that he just didn't know how to fulfill my emotional needs or be a father to me in his younger years. I had stored away my view of him in my hurt pocket for years until listening to Dyer discuss his alcoholic father and how he abandoned his entire family. While on a speaking engagement in Mississippi, Dyer went to his father's grave and at that moment was able to forgive him. The reality was without his father abandoning him, he would have never been able to live out his ultimate mission of being the world's foremost teacher of self-reliance. It was that past hurt that ultimately set the stage and became the inspiration he needed to help himself and in turn help millions of people depend on God and themselves to work through their hard times. If you're going to blame your parents for all the things they didn't do why don't you blame them for all of the things they did do. Because of their actions toward you in the past you have become the person you are today. Because of the "hurt pocket" you can now love deeper, live stronger, give more, and build deeper connections with others that you would never have been able to do if you didn't have this past baggage.

This chapter has been about holes or "missing structures" that you may need to fill. In the next chapter, we will examine why you need to start grieving your lost potential or you will never get serious about playing at a new level. Until you, get frustrated enough to take dramatic action, you will never bust through your current ceiling.

Q AND A WITH COACH BURT

Q: I get the concept of missing structures but what are the most common ones a person could have?

A: In almost every scenario I can go straight to the Whole Person Theory and find a person's missing structures meaning body/ skill, mind/knowledge, heart/passion, and spirit/confidence. Coaching someone in just one of these areas will make a dramatic improvement. With regard to business, the missing structures come down to a poor explanation of services, no selling system, poor follow up, or a passive customer experience.

Q: My kryptonite is a lack of discipline. I have visions but can't seem to get off the fence and manifest them. What do I do?

A: Remember that the word motivation means to take something and see it through to its logical conclusion. It means to become a disciple to your future or vision you see in your mind. A good coach can hold you accountable if you don't have the internal drive to start and finish something or you need some type of consequence. If there's no consequence to your behavior, you won't change until the pain is great enough or the potential is strong enough. There is power in taking action. There is power in momentum. There is power in getting off the fence.

Q: I have a terrible time management problem. What do I do?

A: Time cannot be managed. You have to manage you. This is why I love the time system presented here. I use a planner and map out my most important projects per week via a mental map. The mind doesn't remember things in linear fashion. It remembers pictures. I draw a picture with boxes of my most important tasks in a week. These are only the big rocks. Then every single night I write up my next day. I time block from the moment I wake up until I arrive home at night. I write out my biggest goals of the day. I write out my targets. I seek to get three big wins per day, every day, that are moving my ball down the field toward my dominant focus. Without dominant aspiration, there is no clarity between what is high value use of my time compared to low value use of my time. Once I have my goals in place, I can then ask, "Is this action moving me closer to my dominant aspiration or away from it?" Too many people wake up and waste time on very low value activity all day long that doesn't move them ahead. You don't want to be one of those people.

GRIEVING YOUR LOST POTENTIAL IS WHERE ACTION STARTS

While in Mexico speaking at a 10X event with real estate and sales guru Grant Cardone it hit me. I was listening intently as he explained at when he was 10-year-old, his father died of a massive heart attack. Just a few years later, his older brother died unexpectedly. This sent him to a state of confusion and a lack of certainty about his future. When life hurts, we medicate the pain...with alcohol, drugs, sex or even work, which is almost seen a positive addiction in the U.S. Grant turned to drugs. From age 16 to 25, he was a mess. Even his own family was ashamed of him. At age 25 after a stint in a drug rehab center he decided to get his life together. He became one of the greatest sales people ever but what he said that day caught my attention. He said from ages 25 to 43, he thought he was grieving the loss of his father and brother because that is what every therapist told him. However, when he reached middle age, he came to believe that he was grieving something else, *the loss of all that potential.* All that opportunity that he had squandered. All that impact on the world. All that success that could have affected people. Until that moment in life I had never heard a person say he was grieving lost potential. All that energy and capacity to do good can't be gotten back.

At the end of your life, you may regret many things:

- ▶ You wish you would have spent more time with your family.
- ▶ You wish you wouldn't have worked as hard or spent so many hours in the office.
- ▶ You wish you would have been introduced to God earlier in life.
- ▶ You wish you would have lived the life you really wanted.

I want to add one to the list: I could have. I should have. I was capable of. However, for some reason I didn't. **This is where the grief comes in.** You had all the potential in the world but for whatever reason, you could not activate it. If you're capable of grieving for your lost potential, I believe you can create a new sense of urgency in your life that will propel you to take action instead of talking or merely dreaming.

When I want to awaken an audience that isn't engaged or receptive, I always say, "One of the great hypocrisies of the world is to tell our children as they go off to school in the mornings that they have more potential in the tank, when they are not seeing momma and daddy reach their own." Typically, there is silence and guilt in the room because people recognize this truism. Our children need to see us reaching toward our deepest human potential. They need to see us hustling, pushing, and stretching toward our goals and aspirations. Sadly, the children see the opposite. The parents are playing it safe, uneasy about moving to another city, or afraid to leave smallville to pursue something greater. Growing up in this type of environment sends the children the message that too should believe in playing it safe, avoiding risk and underachieving is acceptable.

This terrible cycle needs to be broken. Consider the following scenario:

1. We start with good intention. It's the new area of your life in which you are underperforming in which you plan to take action on this week.
2. We fail to follow through for various reasons. We are weak minded. We lack discipline. We are comfortable or complacent.
3. We experience ensuing guilt. We grieve our lost potential. We regret our minimal impact.

Now, the guilt makes perfect sense but what are you grieving? You are grieving the actual gap between where you are performing at (your current level) and your real potential. This gap creates grief, which can serve as a powerful motivator to begin taking much bigger actions. Look at it this way:

ACTUAL POTENTIAL

$$\updownarrow \textbf{GAP}$$

CURRENT PERFORMANCE LEVEL

Deep down you know there is a bigger calling for you and your talents. Knowing that you were made to expand and multiply eats away at you if you are not "pursuing your potential." The concept of settling is a "gradual movement into a place of mediocrity." Most people don't settle because they want to but they just allow it to happen. Maybe that's because we've heard that we have a "set point" on our weight, our happiness, our finances and so on. You have to stop thinking that way and start looking at your potential (for life and business) as kinetic energy that is stored until utilized. We hear people make comments like, "Well, a 20% growth year over year is a positive." That's not always a sign of success. Someone might say that measurable success is a winning season or making it into a tournament. However, that's not really success if you could have grown 100%, dominated your competition, or won the championship.

I see us grieving for our lost potential when we wake up and say the following:

- ▶ All my life I've gone for recognition, not impact.
- ▶ All my life I've let others define me in ways that are nonthreatening to them.
- ▶ All my life I've listened to family or friends keep me in a box or tell me not to stretch too far.
- ▶ All my life I've been intimidated by others and I never believed I was as good as the greats.

Potential is relative. It's a mix of knowledge, skills, desire, and confidence, combined with coaching, accountability, and your willingness to push deeper and deeper toward it. You should begin grieving your lost potential if:

1. You waste time and impact because you didn't prepare appropriately.
2. You blow opportunities because you were underprepared.

3. You held back so you didn't hurt other people's feelings.
4. You allowed others to define you.
5. You played small versus went big.

We grieve for lost people, circumstances and things but I believe we should start grieving for our lost potential. Doing so will minimize regret later in life. The most effective way to minimize regret is by taking action. You can never lose because you didn't take action.

How to Become a "Legendary Creature" in Your Space

John Floyd was worth more than $50 million when he hired me to work with him and his company Ole South Properties. A former Kroger manager who began to buy single-family residential homes after watching a late night infomercial, Floyd was proof of the American Dream. Over time, he built the largest independent home building company in Tennessee, selling a startling 777 homes in the early 2000s. In 2009, in the middle of the recession, the company went from selling 40 houses in a week to selling less than four per week. Obviously, this type of decline in business could seriously damage one's confidence, especially when the entire company and your life's passion is at risk. Floyd said to me one day, "When you make a decision to get motivated in your life you make a decision in all areas, not just one." I've never forgotten this line. *He is a legendary creature. He is a Monster.* He went through "The Great Crossover" from being someone who worked at Kroger to a person who solved problems for thousands of people. *You can become this type of person too.*

To become a "legendary creature" you draw the line in the sand of your life and step into the destiny that was preordained for you. (You know that I believe you were formed and knit together for greatness in your mother's womb by God.) It's a matter of carrying out and acting on that belief and on your mission. It may be time for you to decide that you too want to become a "Monster Producer." I like to ask our employees from time to time what it is they really think we do at our company. Several years ago, one employee said, "Do you really want to know the truth of what it is you do for others?" I said, "Absolutely." He took a deep breath and said, "I think you are a freaking monster and you produce other monsters." He went on to say, "I've found a dictionary that says 'a legendary creature that combines multiple skills to dominate.'" When I heard that, I knew our biggest coaching program had just been created. We would call it "Monster Producer" (www.monsterproducer.com). This is a program of likeminded people who aspire to build scalable businesses that impact the world in significant ways. They gather once a month, either in person or online, for coaching from me and top entrepreneurs in my network. This class is full of energy. It's full of ideas. It's full of hustle. It's full of bigger futures. I fully suspect and will speak into vision that this program will be a multi-million dollar division of our company in the next five years.

Like a good Swiss Army knife that can be used to do a variety of tasks, today you must be both versatile and agile. A specialist makes the most money but someone who is a versatile specialist can be extremely valuable. He or she can adjust in different settings, fit in with almost every crowd, and can sell by quickly finding and filling missing structures. In order for you to crossover in your life, you need to recognize these truisms:

1. There is a much bigger future in you and you are tired of solving small problems.
2. There are skills you need to capture to increase your value to the market.

3. There are people from whom you need to seek wisdom and counsel to expand your services.

4. There are people you need to surround yourself with to expand your thinking so you are no longer playing at a local level, but rather at an international level.

5. You are sick and tired of the status quo and ready to break out and become the Monster you know you can be.

Let's break down a strategy that can enable you to completely dominate your backyard before you dominate the whole yard, thus becoming the "must have" in your market versus the "nice to have." I like to use a five-pronged approach to dominate my local market that includes:

 Pick a space and own a clear position.

 Become world-class through real experience doing it.

 Package and sell the process (sell the recipe).

 Overcome obscurity with multiple strategies to get and keep the attention of the audience.

 Completely saturate your local market and box out the competition with mindshare, results, and reputational capital.

STEP 1: PICK A SPACE AND OWN A CLEAR POSITION

Have you ever asked someone what he did for a living or wants to do and the person tells you at least ten things in which he has talent? How can you dominate a space until you pick a position? You may look at your talents and think that you can monetize all of them. You may be able to do so eventually, but narrowing down to your top three is the smarter way to become this Legendary Creature. If you are confused about your space or position, then most likely the market is, as well. To become the best in the world you have to remember the concept of Unique Ability® we discussed earlier in the book. My mind is trained to find another person's unique talents. I can sense it quickly when I listen to his language or watch him work. Usually, this talent was cultivated in someone's past and has been refined and honed over the years.

"What I really do is transform disorganized teams into champions," says Phil Jackson in *Eleven Rings* Bam! How much clearer can you get on what he does? Now, notice why this is so powerful. How many disorganized teams are there in the NBA? How many of their owners want them to be champions? How many of them would pony up the money to become champions?

This is why Jackson can command $12 million per year and handpick which team he wants to coach. You see, this is what defines him as a "legendary creature." He didn't say he owns restaurants, buys real estate, coaches basketball, and on and on. He does one thing better than anyone else: he takes disorganized teams that have never won championships and he unlocks the players' potential in a coordinated and systematic manner with a Zen-like twist. He does that combining his unique experiences, unique mentors and coaches, and que mind-set into an irreplaceable process that makes him the best in the world. He then backs his talent up with his experiences playing in the NBA, coaching in the rookie and international leagues, being an assistant coach, and the other encounters he has had to create a process of "transforming disorganized teams into champions." He has a space and position he owns. What is your space and position?

You can find the answer by asking these questions:

1. What unique talents and abilities do I have that set me apart from others?
2. What unique perspective have I cultivated that differentiates me from other people in my industry?
3. What unique experiences have I had that have set me up to make this "Great Crossover" to play in a much larger arena?
4. What unique process do I have that no one else has that I can package and sell?
5. How do I tell my story or help people get results that will be different from others?

When I was 25 and wrote my first book, *Changing Lives Through Coaching*, I actually wrote it for junior pro coaches. There was no manual when I started a decade earlier and I made tons of mistakes. I wanted to teach other coaches what I had learned the hard way. I probably sold about 50 copies of the book to other coaches but then corporations started to buy the book and asked me to speak. This was in the mid-90s when a "Great Crossover" was starting and companies were urging their managers to become something akin to coaches, especially about attracting, recruiting, retaining and developing talent. Dell Computers invited me to speak to the small business division. At the end of my one-hour presentation, I was given a check, larger than what I made in an entire month coaching high school basketball. My new career had begun. It was in that moment that I figured out I had skills that would transfer to other arenas and I would be compensated in multiples more than my current salary. The magical moment is the moment when you fully realize that the talents that you worked hard to acquire and develop can now be used in multiple arenas. You discover you have a skill set that is unique and differentiated. This is a liberating time that opens your eyes to opportunities that you've never seen before.

You need to accept that you have unique talents that packaged the right way can solve bigger problems and be applicable to other situations. This was what Dan Sullivan said about Unique Ability®. However, until you pick a position in the market, you and the arenas won't understand who you are are, what you do, and why you matter.

STEP 2: BECOME WORLD-CLASS THROUGH THE REAL EXPERIENCE OF DOING IT (PRACTITIONER)

Becoming an expert isn't easy. It only comes after a series of successes and failures, trying and recalibrating, and putting yourself in different scenarios. When I wrote *Person of Interest* I said that you needed seven ingredients and one "free prize" to become a Person of Interest. When you dissect the ingredients shared by all of those experts, it comes down to a combination of these qualities. It's hard for people at the top to articulate what makes them unique or special, so they mention simple things like hard work, willingness to fail, an ability to bounce back, and so forth. They rarely tell you how often they failed, what they learned, how they came back with two strategy changes, how many hours they studied their craft, what their biggest mistakes were, who mentored them, and how they maneuvered through the maze to find the golden ticket at the end. The reason it's hard for them to articulate how to become an expert is because it usually comes down to how they're "wired" to do what needs to be done to complete the job. How can you measure tenacity? How can you measure "want-to" or "emotional quotient" or even "know-how?" How do you measure "killer instinct" or "cheetah-like reflexes?"

Here is the deal: you can't. The reason a person becomes an expert is a combination of all of these qualities; they have the knowledge, skills, desire, and confidence to become people of interest which makes them more interesting and appealing to others.

These people are assets, not liabilities. That may sound like an odd way to view people when in fact this is what people think about when they meet new people.

Think of **an asset** as something that:

- ▶ Adds something.
- ▶ Adds energy.
- ▶ Adds money.
- ▶ Adds time.
- ▶ Adds creativeness, trust, chemistry, knowledge, expertise, and speed—"intangible" or "invisible" assets.

A liability:

- ▶ Subtracts something.
- ▶ Subtracts time.
- ▶ Subtracts money.
- ▶ Subtracts energy.
- ▶ Subtracts confidence.

The faster you can prove that you are an asset the faster someone will seek you out instead of another option. I call this "The Immediate Asset." In today's fast-paced world in the "current of the urgent" it is vital that you prove to others FAST that you are an immediate asset. This means that through just ONE interaction the other person can tell immediately tell that you can help him. *You are interesting and intriguing.* You show that you can immediately add something that the person isn't accustomed to receiving. Many people take six meetings and six months to show they can be an asset. My strategy is to become one in the first five minutes or first 15 seconds if possible.

Becoming a "Must-Have" versus a "Nice to Have"

You need to be a "must-have" versus a "nice to have." The latter are cut during recessions and down revenue years. Must-haves are never cut. *They are invaluable.* Here is how you ramp up your "must-have" factor:

1. Think "specialist" not "generalist." Think heart surgeon versus general practitioner. My younger brother had a bad accident at work and almost lost his thumb. He was transported him to Vanderbilt University Hospital, where a plastic surgeon who specialized in hands was brought in because he was the best. What specialty area do you bring to the equation?

2. Solve majors problem through your talents, knowledge, or creativity that no one else can solve. When you solve major problems with your skill set, you get paid big money.

3. Create a unique, differentiated, and original point of view. Covey used to say, "When two opinions are the same, then one of those opinions is unnecessary." If you are saying the same thing everyone says, then why do people need you? Must-haves are so valuable because their point of view is clearly differentiated and unique. You want these people "in the room" when big decisions are made.

4. Get results that others simply cannot get. Results always speak for themselves, and when your results are superior to your direct competitors and marketed appropriately, then others will seek you out.

5. Become well known, or celebrated in your niche. Then, you become the go-to person and the "person of interest," which means an in-demand person of influence others are seeking out.

How Do You Know When You are Becoming a "Must-Have?"

1. People want an "exclusive" partnership with you and will agree to sign a non-compete agreement and not work with your competitors because they believe you are the one person in your space that they want on their team.
2. You ask for and get the fees you want without any negotiations.
3. There is high demand from a very specific client list.
4. You are picking and choosing with whom you work.
5. When budgets are cut, you are not cut although others are let go.

How Do You Know When You are a "Nice to Have?"

1. You are constantly having to fight for relevance and importance to the hierarchy.
2. You are constantly having to negotiate your fees because clients don't see the perceived value which you believe you are providing.
3. When you help clients get superior results they attribute them to good markets, other variables, and just natural growth without giving you any credit.
4. You have to take on every client who calls because demand for your service is very low.
5. The word "budget" comes up in discussions with clients so you feel that you're on the chopping block.

Your goal is to always become INVALUABLE to those you serve. This will insulate you from competitors, provides future job security, and allow you to live from abundance versus scarcity. If you begin to detect that your value is diminishing or you are becoming obsolete, think back to the difference between an asset and liability and search for ways to create more money, energy, results, or relevance. Some of the firms where I've coached and consulted have brought me back after many years. That's because I constantly evolve my skill sets and try to find new ways to add new value. I try to show my relevance by becoming an asset and tackling all major problems that need solving.

I try to become what I write about in *Person of Interest*. People of Interest are always in demand and considered "must-haves." Look at the **Person of Interest** (POI) prism on the opposite page to visualize the attributes you need to be the expert in the field.

Look at this grid and ask one question: what am I lacking to become the PERCEIVED expert in our space? It may be hard to admit that you lack certain ingredients and it may take the help of someone (your coach) to help articulate what you are missing, but most likely when you find and fill these missing structures your POI score will go up and you will start being perceived as the expert.

STEP 3: PACKAGE AND SELL THE PROCESS (SELL THE RECIPE VS. BAKE THE CAKE)

Part of becoming an expert is learning how to package and sell your intellectual property. This is just a fancy way of saying, "How do you take what is in your mind and put it into something others can consume?" Many people refer to this as "packaging," but they are often undercapitalized in this arena.

Become a
PERSON OF INTEREST

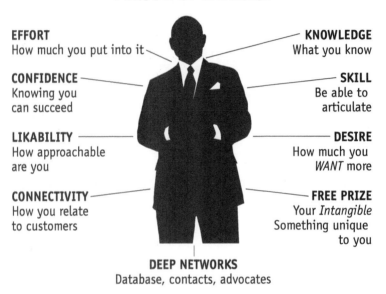

EFFORT
How much you put into it

CONFIDENCE
Knowing you
can succeed

LIKABILITY
How approachable
are you

CONNECTIVITY
How you relate
to customers

KNOWLEDGE
What you know

SKILL
Be able to
articulate

DESIRE
How much you
WANT more

FREE PRIZE
Your *Intangible*
Something unique
to you

DEEP NETWORKS
Database, contacts, advocates

For example, I used a local real estate agent on one of my rental properties. The day I said I was going to use her, she went out to the property and placed a sign in the yard saying "coming soon." She then lined up a person to rehab the property (without asking me, by the way). She already has taken the initiative and has been a cheetah in doing so. In less than three days, she had four competing offers on the property. Here is the problem: her cheetah mind-set and actions are nowhere to be found in her marketing. What she has is a "packaging" and "marketing" problem. She needs to take that process and her mind-set and articulate it to the market in a way that the consumer can easily understand what makes her unique. Without doing this, she is quickly commoditized with the other real estate agents in her market, and in the eyes of the consumer, she is no different or better than they are.

Think of packaging in this way:

This book packages my expertise to share it with you in a way that is easy to understand and use. All the years of coaching, all the wins, all the books, and all the failures are of no value to you unless I can package them in a way that you can consume them. I could also package this intellectual property into other consumable creations such as podcasts, workshops and coaching programs, licensing plays, TV and radio, and speaking engagements. Think of multiple profit centers that are driven by your thought processes. We like to generate multiple revenue sources off one concept or idea. Look at the diagram on the opposite page to see what I mean. Then, consider how you can drive more profit centers from one concept or division of your company.

In this case, we took one concept and packaged it into multiple profit centers. I learned this many years ago when I spent time with David Hoyt, the agent for Dr. John Maxwell, the leadership author and former pastor who has sold more than 40 million books. Hoyt showed me how his team "packaged and sold" Maxwell's ideas into six to eight concepts. Once I learned this strategy, I became aware of how an image, hook, subtitles or position statements either increase your brand value or diminish

it. I also learned that in fact, Maxwell does not write his own books; Charlie Wetzel does. Maxwell promotes and speaks what Wezel writes and together they sold millions of books. We all should aspire to find relationships like this one that position partners in their strength zones so they both win.

If you do not own a company, you may be asking, "What does this have to do with me?" Well, know this, **you are a brand**. Your packaging includes your appearance, clothing, explanation of services, ability to articulate your special offerings, your follow-up, and your response time. I see people wearing outdated clothing, sending bad resumes, and not being able to have an articulate conversation. If you can't package and sell your skills, then you will always be underperforming financially. Your packaging is DIRECTLY tied to your compensation. Robert Kiyosaki, author of the wildly popular *Rich Dad, Poor Dad* always said, "Outdated wardrobes equal outdated mindsets." Think of packaging as anything a consumer, employer or anyone can see, feel, touch, or taste. If it screams rookie or not talented, be prepared for small results.

STEP 4: OVERCOME OBSCURITY WITH MULTIPLE STRATEGIES TO GET AND KEEP ATTENTION OF THE AUDIENCE

I believe the primary problem any talented person has is simple: **Obscurity**. Obscurity is when you have the goods—you may even be the best in the world—but not enough people know who you are, or they know you but can't figure out how you specifically can help them. Consequently, you and your brand are obscure. The actors we see on TV are there because they put themselves in a position to overcome obscurity. They moved to Hollywood. They got in front of directors. They got agents. They went from being "unknown" to "known." This is really your job. When the most renowned leadership expert, John Maxwell, came to speak in my hometown, I dined with him in the most popular restaurant. No one knew who he was I watched as he greeted people and started conversations, and by the time he left, everyone was asking, "Who was that man?" This gave me the opportunity to say, "That was John Maxwell, one of the top leadership experts in the world."

We all fight obscurity. It's our job to take our message and talents to the world and get as much attention as we can. Look at this formula:

- ▶ People do business with people whom they know and respect.
- ▶ If I don't know you, how can I respect you?

▶ If I don't know or respect you (packaging), then what is
the likelihood I would ever do business with you?

The first step is to get my attention and then articulate how
you can be an asset, not a liability to me.

Getting attention in a world of social media, 24/7 news cycles
and instant global communication is incredibly difficult. My
strategy is simple: dominate the backyard before you dominate
the whole yard. To do this I use a number of strategies to build
"brand awareness." There is a difference between "brand awareness" and "brand insistence." I operate from a simple premise
when it comes to marketing. Marketing is what you do to get
your phone to ring. Selling is what you do when it does ring. I
also believe in the philosophy of marketing so people will see
your name everywhere. This ties into the concept of being omni-
present and cultivates brand reputational capital and social proof
of energy and action.

Here are seven strategies we currently use to enhance brand
awareness:

1. *Showcase marketing events on a consistent basis*—These
   are events we either host or where I speak for no fee to
   get in front of "economic buyers." This gives an audience
   a chance to "sample the goods" before they buy and to
   get them excited about the product.

2. *Social media*—We use every social media platform
   in a key way. I believe social media platforms are not
   for selling but to turn you into becoming a **Person of
   Interest** attractive to the market. What you are really
   selling is your "point of view" and you're trying to attract
   other people who believe the same things you do. I run
   every post I make through a lens of "what does someone

reading this get?" If I don't think people will get some value, then I don't post it. Social media consumption is for them, not you.

3. *Weekly newspaper key spots*—I don't advertise in the local paper but I do write a weekly editorial in the business section that goes out to more than 100,000 people. This gives me another "touch point" so I'm visible in my local market.

4. *Graffiti ads*—These are ads placed in high-end restaurants that we use to elevate status. They reach a captive audience, allowing me to brand myself with my position in the market of "Everybody needs a Coach in Life." This is just a touch point.

5. *Database and text message system*—I like frequency and high touch. Our database allows us to gather key information about people and "touch" them on a consistent basis by either an e-mail or a text message. I write my own copy and make sure what I have to say is interesting and not selling. I want to remind them I'm available and offer solutions to their problems.

6. *Podcasts and interviews*—I like the podcast strategy. We've created our own weekly show called "Super Coach" that has thousands of listeners from around the world. We also live stream this to our own network (www.greatnessnetwork.com) and to iTunes and other podcast platforms. This gives us additional content for reputational capital and allows us to attract many other people. I also regularly join other top podcasts as a guest to leverage their audiences.

7. Weekly blogging—Some believe that the blog is dead.
   I disagree. I use www.medium.com and LinkedIN to
   pump out 2- to 10-minute quick reads and use these
   posts for my various distribution channels. The topic
   needs to be a SEXY since people make a decision to read
   or delete in less than 2.7 seconds. Give them something
   interesting to read.

Most people are relying on way too few strategies to overcome obscurity. Remember, you have a song to sing and there is
an audience waiting to hear it. It is your job to take your show on
the road and get attention. Why do you think artists go on tour
or authors speak? It has solely to get attention for their brand.
These events are where they make the most money. As long as
you remain obscure, you are drastically limiting your future and
opportunities.

STEP 5: COMPLETELY SATURATE YOUR LOCAL MARKET AND BOX OUT THE COMPETITION WITH MINDSHARE, RESULTS, AND REPUTATIONAL CAPITAL

In the back of everyone's mind is a tiny piece of real estate owned
by someone. That piece of real estate only has room for one key
expert. And you want that one key expert to be YOU. So the
question becomes how do we own that piece of real estate and
dominate the mindshare of all of those in your market? It comes
down to phrases:

- ▸ **Top of mind**
- ▸ **Constant frequency**

If you understand anything about the laws of attraction, you
know that someone can be attracted to you in the morning but

can completely forget you by the afternoon. It's called "object impermanence" and is often seen in young children. The reason we HAVE to keep people's attention is because loyalty is fleeting and you have to dominate people's thoughts in order to keep their attention. Remember that money follows attention. Money follows energy. Money follows action. Money follows circulation.

Where there is no energy or action, there is no business. Use the strategy of "I see your name everywhere," in your local market because this is how you will saturate the market and everyone's mindshare. Aim to get as high touch and as high frequency as you can in every way that you can. I do this through my Top 25 strategy where I cultivate 25 deep and meaningful relationships with people who are influencers. They help me spread the message and support me even when I'm not there. I'm not there. I also do this by circulating my message. This is why your "campaign speech" is so essential. You need to share it over and over again until you have beat the drum so frequently that people can't help but listen.

When you take this approach, you will get attention. You will also attract some criticism and possibly some haters. In the end, as Grant Cardone says, "You will get admiration."

Know this: winning is a game of probability. If you want to increase the odds dramatically in your favor, then you have to get off the bench and into the game. The "Great Crossover" is about making two jumps: one in your mind to sell yourself to yourself and one in the mind of the public, so people begin to take you seriously as a real contender. Until this crossover happens, you'll remain the minors, solving very small problems and getting very small returns.

In today's saturated and ultra-competitive market, there's never been a better time to cultivate an "unfair advantage" and an "inch of separation." In the next chapter, I'll show you how your coach could be where your ENTIRE competitive advantage comes from.

Q AND A WITH COACH BURT

Q: I feel myself becoming complacent and don't have the drive to become a "Legendary Creature." What can I do?

A: In my experiences, only a small percentage of the population aspires to become legendary. This 1% stretches, strives and are never satisfied. They want more. They grieve their lost potential. They dominate markets and don't rely on the good opinion of others. They want impact vs. recognition. Either you have this gene or you don't. You may be able to acquire it but by the tone of your question, you may need to accept that you can have a good life of good impact but you may never get to the great level.

Q: I'm having a hard time picking a position because I'm good at and interested in many things. How do I narrow it down?

A: I suffer from this one too and know this problem well. Let me put it to you this way. If you were giving one Ted Talk of 18 minutes that millions of people would see and you were talking about only ONE thing in which you were the expert, what would it be? For me it would be "Why everybody needs a coach in life." Yes, I can do other things but my core essence is I am the preeminent expert on coaching. Think about whether you could say you are the world's #1 expert in the world in one subject. You need to move away from your various activities and expend all your resources and capacity into this one field.

Q: I have a packaging problem. I am that real estate agent who is good but can't seem to communicate it to the world in a way that elevates my business. What do I do?

A: Well, all progress starts by telling the truth. Once you find what makes you unique and differentiated, you have to "distribute" that talent to the world in the form of marketing. Think of marketing as taking what you have and getting it to the people who need and want it the most. Packaging is anything people can see, touch, taste, smell, or consume. Your website, appearance, car, flyer, listing presentation or anything else you give out is part of your packaging and either raises your brand value or diminishes it. The best packaging explains what you do, how you do it differently, and puts a bow around your product or service to serve it up to exactly to those who need and want it. This is why consistency, what you put on Facebook, and your reputational capital, is so critical. Many small business owners and solopreneurs don't take the time needed to package themselves and consequently they always stay small.

CREATING AN UNFAIR
ADVANTAGE IN A
COMMODITIZED WORLD

One of my most meaningful coaching assignments in my career started in a workshop attended by only three people. After a long day, my assistant begged me to cancel it but I said to her, "If these people paid their money then we will give them their money's worth." That is exactly what we did. Always remember that every day in your current role is an interview for your next role. Every day with your current customer is an interview for your next customer. That night I taught from my best-selling book *This Ain't No Practice Life: Go from where you are to where you want to be* as if I was performing at Madison Square Garden. One of those three people just happened to be the CEO of a $40 million company and she was picking up what I was putting down, if you know what I mean. On the first break she said, "This is exactly what we've been looking for," which happened to be a personal growth plan and coaching program for her 200-plus employees. We began a conversation that would lead me to a four-year process in one of the most unlikely fields in the world, the adult prison system in the state of Tennessee.

Yes, you read that correctly. I said the *prison system*. As you are probably aware, there is a major problem in this country related to the rehabilitation of those who end up in prison. The failing cycle typically proceeds in this order:

1. You are a loner with very little confidence or direction, so you link up with others similar to you (with little or no direction). You also have no real coach in your life who will hold you accountable.
2. You get into trouble by committing a crime against society.
3. You get caught and end up in prison.
4. You do your time and we hope you get rehabilitated through some type of transformational experience (you find God, someone walks into your life, you change).
5. Many times this doesn't happen.
6. Ninety-eight percent of those who go to prison get out.
7. A large number of these people go right back to doing whatever caused them to get into prison the first time because they have little confidence, few friends, no strong support system, no real skills, no driver's license, and no money. They have very little opportunity to change their future.

In the end, guess who has the privilege of paying for this cycle? We all do. We spend double the amount we spend on education on our prison systems! Surely, there has to be a better way. That night at my event, we had a vision: What if the offender had a coach who was in charge of "accelerating" the rehabilitation and transformation process? Guess what? I was brought in to do exactly this job: coach the coaches, or in this case, take "supervisors" and transition them to "coaches" who can develop the raw talent and potential in those who had committing crimes against society. And I had a blast.

After more than four years and more than 84 hours of coaching directly from me, we had successfully coached, trained, and certified more than 200 employees who would be interacting with thousands of offenders. We certified a group of "master coaches" who would focus on the sustainability of the content, and we went to work. Every offender participating in this program would have a coach who would help them grow them in four core areas:

1. *Knowledge* for the mind
2. *Skills* for the body
3. *Desire* for the heart
4. *Confidence* for the spirit

Sound familiar? Yes, ***every offender needs a coach in life*** too, and that is exactly what they got. Each week they watched a short video of me explaining the seven core decisions they needed to make to transform their lives. Then their "supervisor," now their coach, began to work with them in both group and one-to-one meetings. This cycle is continues for 32 weeks and is then repeated. We believe this will drastically improve the mission's success rate of "get them out and keep them out."

You may be thinking that this is fascinating but has nothing to do with gaining an advantage in the market? Actually, I use it to illustrate a point. What if you had a lazy coach while in prison? What if you had a coach who didn't pay attention during my trainings? What if you had an apathetic coach? Wouldn't this set you up to fail compared to your fellow offenders? However, on the other hand, what if you had an incredibly insightful, energetic, and knowledgeable coach who became your secret weapon? What if daily, weekly, monthly, and even yearly your coach "fed his sheep" in a regular and systematic manner that grew your knowledge, kill, desire, and confidence? What if you were able to get out of prison and accelerate your life all because of your coach? I believe your entire competitive advantage could come from one place: your coach.

It Was a SAD Day...

One of the saddest days of my coaching career was when I had to "cut" players. A 14-year-old girl would come in with passion and desire to make our basketball team. She had been playing from the time she was four or five years old. She stayed up late at night practicing with her dad in the driveway with hopes of one day playing for the Lady Warriors. Many times, we begin watching, scouting, and spending time with children and their families as early as the fourth grade.

What happened to that teen who I had to cut from the team? She was usually deficient in one of four areas:

1. Knowledge of the game
2. Skills to execute on the knowledge
3. Desire to do the inconvenient at the highest level
4. Confidence to take advantage of the kind of coaching you need to advance

The parents would come to seem me after I posted the "made it" list on the outside of the door. They would be furious and looking for an answer. Once they calmed down, they would start rationalizing, "But Coach, she has been playing from the time she was four." I would then say, "I know. This breaks my heart to tell you this but she has been playing for the wrong people." I would then say, "Most likely, she had a bad coach in junior pro followed up by a poor coach in elementary ball followed by another unqualified coach in middle school. Because of this poor coaching she is simply are not equipped to play for us that this time." Often, the kids weren't at fault. The blame belonged with the parents and coaches. The parents' job was to put their children in an environment where they could expand their skills. It was the coaches' job to cultivate the necessary know-how so the players could advance to the next level, not just win games in peewee leagues. This type of poor coaching always catches up with you.

I liked when players came to me with "batteries included." They knew the game, had the know-how, cultivated the mental toughness, and had been battle-tested through appropriate competition. In other words, they had an advantage because what their prior coaches had taught them. This same concept translates completely to the business.

Now, I introduce Ram Charan to you. The concept of becoming "famous" is something I teach in *Person of Interest*. Famous means known, renown, or celebrated. It's when more people know you than you know them. You become famous in life for just a few things including:

- ▶ The results you achieve personally or the ones you help others achieve.
- ▶ Your "point of view" that is clearly differentiated from everyone else's.

- ▸ Your "talent" that is unique in a world of sameness.
- ▸ Becoming "infamous" for getting in trouble or not being mainstream or normal.

One evening while flying in from Chicago I thought I recognized Ram Charan, a "famous person" in the leadership space, on the plane. Being the nerd that I am, I realized that no one else in the airport recognized him. I wandered over to him and said, "Can I have your autograph, as I'm a big fan?" He said yes and signed his name on a napkin. Then, two armed security guards whisked him into a private car that waiting outside the door. It then struck me. Ram, one of the most well known business consultants in the world, was in Nashville to work with a growing company. He was so VALUABLE to the executives that they wanted him to be protected. He was their "secret weapon." He was their "unfair advantage." How valuable would you have to be for a client to want to protect you?

As a die-hard basketball fan and former championship women's coach I watched how the beloved Pat Summitt stepped away from the very program she had led to so many championships because of her dementia. Unfortunately, her success has not been replicated since her departure. For the first time in decades, Lady Vols dropped out of the women's college basketball top 25. Summitt was the team's "unfair advantage."

To become the one who is a client's "secret weapon" or "unfair advantages" you need to:

1. Make yourself so valuable and provide such a competitive advantage for the companies you work for that they would want to protect you like Ram Charan.
2. Find your own coach who can provide such a competitive advantage that you might consider asking for a

non-compete clause so the person only works with you. Those who are the best are the most awarded and coveted.

Separation in a Same World

I believe there has never been a better time to look different, run faster, and be agile. We talk about this in our book, *Zebras and Cheetahs.* Nine out of ten people do not even understand that they need to separate themselves from their competitors and find a differentiator. Instead, they compete with the same products and services, the same language, and the same old mind-set everybody else is using.

A coach is the third party—the impartial observer—who can draw out the distinctions in your work. After all, there are more than one million real estate agents, more than 285,000 financial advisors, and more than 100,000 mortgage originators. There are little or no differences among the people in these highly competitive markets. We desperately need to think in terms of differentiation and distinction.

I believe you can separate yourself from your competitors if:

1. **Your product or service is BETTER than your competitors' are.** Think YETI or APPLE. I once worked with a bank that offered a 6% interest rate on a checking account. It was easy to sell and easy to dominate the competition because of the clear advantage of this product. Very few companies can win in this category, especially if they are selling someone else's product that is distributed to multiple outlets.
2. **Your DELIVERY of the same product or service is better.** I just returned from Mexico, where I stayed at

a five-star resort. I then flew back home and stayed at a Courtyard by Marriott. The service level of the same product (lodging) was not even remotely comparable. The five-star resort thought of everything imaginable a guest might want or need and provided it. On the other hand, the Marriott closed down its bistro at lunch, when people were hungry. You can win on the same product with better and more structured service and a service culture that exceeds the demands and expectations of the consumer.

3. **Your POINT of VIEW, PERSPECTIVE, and MIND-SET are far better than others are.** Why can Nick Saban at Alabama develop football talent better than Les Miles at LSU? How does Phil Jackson outcoach Del Harris? It is how they think, respond, create, extract, and deliver on a promise. If you're working in very saturated markets, your clear differential advantage, your X Factor, will be you. Your biggest challenge will be either duplicating you or scaling you. Trust me, I have played this game and it is easier than it sounds. Why do you think that APPLE University has one goal: teach people how to THINK and RESPOND like Steve Jobs? He was the company's competitive advantage.

How you think, respond, create, extract, and deliver on a promise comes from what you learn from your coach. The three years I spent with Dan Sullivan's Strategic Coach® program gave me the structures and systems that clearly provided a competitive advantage in my market. It was not my products or services but rather my point of view that would differentiate my service.

Your greatest investment and asset is YOU. If you hone your raw undeveloped talent and skills each step of the way, you will dominate those who are too lazy to get coached, too frugal to pay for coaching, or too undisciplined to act on what they learned.

Your Place of DISTINCTION Could Be in One Place: Your Ability to EXTRACT, SYNTHESIZE, and SHARE

This realization came while I was at an XO marriage conference in Southlake, Texas, at one of the largest churches in the United States called Gateway. I bet that you will have your revelation at some point because someone has been pressing you for it or perhaps you have been trying to find your true gift in life. After several hours at the marriage conference where I listened to other couples articulate their differences and then applied their concepts to at least four other things going on in my head (including my marriage), I knew exactly what my gift was: the gift of **EXTRACTION**. Extraction (from my perspective) is the ability to hear, see, absorb, or experience something and IMMEDIATELY see its applicability to another arena, and then implement it there. It is the ability to read a book and give an entire presentation on it the next day. The gift of extraction is related to the gift of **RETENTION**, the ability to sift through, absorb, and retain large amounts of information at an accelerated pace. Therefore, when it comes to distinguishing yourself from your competitors, you must first find and explore this gift, which could come from any of these areas:

- ▶ Hardwired from an early age by the creator and coming naturally to you, then refined over the course of your life.
- ▶ Experiences which placed you in various situations that exposed your gifts.

- ▸ Struggles you've had in the past which helped you to utilize your gift to rectify a bad situation.
- ▸ Formal or informal education which have given you a competitive advantage over your peers and competitors today.
- ▸ Special coaching which has provided accelerated insights into strategy, thought processes, execution, or bounce-back tactics.

I first noticed this "gift" of extraction at age 19 when I read *The 7 Habits of Highly Effective People: Powerful Lessons in Personal Change* by Stephen Covey. I immediately begin to teach these seven habits to all of my players as another means to build a "competitive intelligence." It was then that I could explain my unique gifting as a coach; I understood that I have a unique capacity to "inner engineer" people to win from the inside out. Because I'm able to do this quickly, I often help people speed up this process, which could take them years on their own.

You have to identify your ONE gift that you exploit, nourish and refine until you become the best in the world. This gift then becomes the SINGLE place where you win. I like to tell people that I cannot beat Tony Robbins, John Maxwell, or even Grant Cardone head to head with my brand versus theirs. They have 30 more years of experience than me. However, the one place where I can beat them is in my life experiences of extracting, synthesizing, and delivering "coaching content." I can beat them in my space because I'm a coach who has actually won a championship. You have to find the one space that you can own when competing.

God bestowed the talent upon me of extraction. What gifting did you receive and are you doing anything with it?

2.2mm of Strategy Change Could Be Your Differential Advantage

I like to use the analogy that a good plastic surgeon rarely makes more than 2.2 mm of change and never more than seven changes. You most likely do not need to overhaul your whole life or entire business to see some kind of significant output or advantage. What you need are two small changes that could have a significant impact on your business. Always remember this saying: "You can 2x your business by just working harder but you could never 10x your business by working harder." *This is a strategy problem.* Here is the issue: we are creatures of habit that we literally just hit the repeat button on all our approaches year after year. We make very few changes in our strategy from one year to the next. We might show a small shift—5% to 10%—but we never show quantum changes. I set my targets to expand by as much as 100% year over year. This stretches me. This pushes me. This expands me. To accomplish this, we have to change our strategy, not our work ethic. In many years, I actually worked less and earned more by making only two small changes in our strategy. Here are several examples of how this 2.2 mm of change strategy we implemented in my company and in my personal life can open big doors:

> ▸ In 2015, we wired our "Greatness Factory" (a unique destination for people from all occupations who have made a personal decision to become great) so we could "live stream" or simulcast our training programs to anyone anywhere via WebEx. This subscription program only costs us only $79 per month and less than $700 for the equipment. With this technology, we can serve customers ANYWHERE, allowing our sales teams to make global sales so individuals can participate in live

training sessions from their offices or homes. This small modification had a significant impact. Think of small changes you can make for less than $1,000 that could open similar opportunities for you.

▶ In 2016, we introduced Talent Supply, a program that coaches your new hires or underperformers for a 90-day cycle. This helps them build the necessary skills they need to be successful on day 91. The participants are required to make one hour's worth of phone calls to prospects or clients while getting training so they're still doing their jobs. They also receive more than 84 hours of training from Bruce Lund, my #2 coach. He is teaching the class instead of me. This small adjustment has opened up an entirely new market allowing us to sell more programs **to our existing clients, and enabling us to offer an additional service that solves an under-served need**. By offering programs for new staff as well as middle and top performers as well as managers, we have become a one-stop shop for a company's training needs—and we increase our revenue. You may be able to provide a service related to your current offerings by finding and solving a client problem. You uncover these problems by listening; I kept hearing leaders say, "We need a better onboarding plan for our new hires and we need new sales people to produce faster."

▶ In 2016, we developed Monster Operations to work solely with operations teams to find out what structures they were missing. These team typically get the least amount of attention but can sometimes provide the most valuable and competitive advantage to a company since they are the ones "delivering" on the promise to the consumer. Every company has sales and operations and often there is a missing link between the two groups. With Monster Operations, we now can work with the sales, management, and operations teams, allowing us to cross-sell to our clients and offer valuable solutions. This expands the range of our services and multiplies the size of our contracts. Again, we are simply finding client problems and taking the initiative to provide solutions. The more valuable we can become the more likely they will view us as a "must have," not a "nice to have" service.

► In 2016, we collaborated with LightSpeed Virtual Training, the most comprehensive online training company in the world, led by my friend Brad Lea. This allows us to build "Coach Burt's Total Growth Academy" and sell "off the shelf" virtual training to anyone or any company that wants virtual training. Employees can log in daily and get coaching on EVERY imaginable topic including sales, leadership, entrepreneurship, operations, and 90 day sales training. With more than 20 different programs on success for each segment of the company's operations, I believe we have the most inclusive online program in the world. This allows us to offer an affordable product ($249 to $399 monthly for a year commitment) we can sell off the shelf. This investment helps us scale the company, gives our sales team a product rather than a service to sell, and expands our product line which ultimately increases our revenue. Again, we already had the content but that 2.2 mm of change strategy to open up new opportunities for us.

▶ In 2016, I developed a fear of flying. It was odd because I have flown all over the world in two-seater planes and in Airbuses, so I couldn't understand why all of a sudden this fear was paralyzing me. It was primarily a fear of closed off spaces. I specifically did not want to fly on small planes and rearranged all of my flights to be on 737 or larger planes which forced me to find cities with international airports and then drive, sometimes for hours, to get to my destination. Part of my 2.2 mm of strategy change was to begin looking for people to help me overcome this debilitating fear. I found my person in Pastor Jimmy Evans of Texas who has a weekly show called Marriage Today. He preaches about fighting fear. I would listen to his sermons at night before going to bed and once I heard him say, "You cannot have two thoughts simultaneously. When you have fear replace that thought immediately." I was speaking in New Haven, Connecticut to financial advisors and needed to return to Knoxville to present to another group the next morning; I had no choice but to take a small 20-seat propeller DC-8. I was terrified but I remembered Jimmy's words. I bought a small fan to keep air on my face. I plugged in my headphones (to his podcast, of course, on "Changing your mind on worry and fear") and I read and watched shows to watch on my MacBook. I kept busy and wouldn't you know, I made it without any problems and actually enjoyed the experience (no long lines, easy boarding and departure and actually bigger seats). My 2.2 mm strategy shift was to replace my thoughts about "fear of flying" by staying occupied and adding distractions. These were simple but powerful strategies.

These are all strategy moves, not effort moves. Notice I did not say that our 2.2 mm of strategy change was going to be that we would start at 6 a.m. and work until 10 p.m. I didn't say we would hire new staffers. Instead, I am constantly looking for an inch of separation and small changes that can have a major impact.

In 2015, one of my favorite real estate agents increased her production from $50 million to $65 million. She did not overhaul her entire business. She did not hire many new people or get fancier offices. She merely added ONE key relationship with a builder and that relationship brought her 73 more deals and $15 million in revenue. This is a great example of a 2.2 mm of change in strategy that yields big results.

Stop right now and think about the 2.2 mm of strategy change you will be implementing in the next year. What small change would make a HUGE difference in your business? You will be surprised that when you start thinking this way, your life will get much easier. We are hardwired to win by brute force and we then work harder but not smarter. Think about what I said at the start of this book: the "current of the urgent" or the "whirlwind" that allows us no time to decompress. We just hit repeat over and over, which produces small incremental changes. That is not what you want; you are aiming for the quantum leap I have been discussing throughout this book.

Are you hungry enough to take action and formulate this 2.2mm of strategy improvement? I often tell people trying to break through a ceiling: ***Satisfied needs never motivate people, only unsatisfied needs.***

Q AND A WITH COACH BURT

Q: I understand that I need to differentiate but I don't know how to do this. Can you help me?

A: We live in a highly competitive world where there is a lot of copying and very little innovation. Consider whether you have a distinct advantage over your competitors. To determine this, you will have to study them and their products inside and out, and begin to find small ways to set you apart. This could come from a product that you build to be different (think Tesla), the form of your delivery of your product (think Chick-Fil-A), or YOU because of some unique quality you have to offer. Therefore, we must find the advantage and then we must articulate through marketing and EOS your advantage. It is our job to find what makes us distinctive and sell the heck out of that feature.

Q: When you say we live in a commoditized world what do you mean?

A: There are literally millions of professionals in every industry. Commoditized means saturated, same, without a differential advantage. If all the products and services are the same, then most people will just pick the cheapest one. To avoid playing that game, you need to create unique and proprietary value so you can charge more and break out of the commodity game. Very few people understand this so that is why so many are competing for the same attention in the same space, and the same game.

Q: I've always believed that I could just work my way into wining more but you are saying that I could have a strategy problem. How do I drastically expand my business?

A: Studies show that people who are world class don't just work harder than their peers do; they work much harder. This means their intensity, tenacity, practice, and the failures they have are astounding compared to non-performers. For example, a study of top violinists showed that they practiced three times more than non-professionals did even though it was the least enjoyable thing they did. This speaks to their drive and commitment. I believe you can increase your business twofold by coming in later and working harder but you will never be able to increase it tenfold. You will always do more by shifting the 2.2mm to bring a new offering to the market or sell to a new audience. I suggest looking at your strategies to see which can deliver the maximum output with less input on your part. Stop believing that if you make more calls or work harder you will get there.

5

THE "COACH-EPRENEUR" CREATED FROM THE UNION OF BUSINESS AND SPORTS

I believe there is a connection between the knowledge and skills of the great athletic coaches and the knowledge and skills of the great business minds. It is a merger between the boardroom and the locker room. This coming-together is producing a new kind of coach and leader, someone who is part coach, part entrepreneur, and all leader. I call this person a coach-epreneur. If you are currently CEO but have not already done so, I predict you will shift your leadership approach to start following the acumen of these new coach-epreneurs.

This new kind of coach knows the difference between an asset and a liability and understands how to take lower-level resources to higher levels of productivity. In my athletic coaching days, I borrowed ideas from the corporate arena and brought them back to the sports world. Now, as a business and entrepreneurial coach, I do the same thing. I borrow the intensity, the mind-set of champions, and the systematic approach we used in sports to win and in the corporate arena. If you are looking to hire a coach, you want someone who possesses these skills and if you are a leader or a coach yourself, you may need to expand your arsenal of coaching weapons.

Great athletic coaches know how to:

1. Study the market consistently (their competitors) and exploit their weaknesses.
2. Spend hours dissecting their teams and placing their players in a position where they can create the most value.
3. Make necessary adjustments at a moment's notice and not remain stuck using old tired ideas that no longer work.
4. Give harsh and immediate feedback to their teams and have "critical conversations."
5. Systematically attack the competition with a real game plan that has multiple options, which you can deploy immediately without having to wait until "next year" to start an initiative.
6. Motivate the unmotivated.
7. Control momentum with various strategies.

Great entrepreneurs and business minds know how to:

1. Quickly recognize an asset from a liability.
2. Take lower-level resources and convert them to higher-level resources.
3. Market and promote their products and services at very high levels.

4. Raise capital needed to expand, grow, and multiply.
5. Take risks that others typically would not take.
6. Penetrate new markets to avoid being stagnant.
7. Try multiple ideas and consistently recalibrate those that do not work.

A select few Super Coaches such as John Calipari, the University of Kentucky men's basketball coach, understand all these needs. He knows the new era coach must recruit and attract better talent, coach and develop that talent, and get the most out of those players. He also knows that to attract better players he must market and exploit the strengths of his program, articulate a clear message to the fans and alumni, and manage a budget of several million dollars like a CEO.

The Coach-eprenur must also have versatility. For some, I'm their life coach; for some, I'm their strategist; for some I'm their business coach; and for some, I'm their sales coach. One day I may be working with people who crawl underneath a house to fix your air conditioning unit or spray for bugs, and the next day I may meet with financial advisors who earn more than $1 million per year. The new coach is not one-dimensional. Remember earlier when I said Steve Jobs took a walk every Sunday with his business coach Bill Campbell. I bet there were times Bill was Jobs' life coach, not simply his business coach. His job was to help Jobs gain clarity and confidence in all aspects of life. Marcus Lemonis, CEO of Camping World and star of the CNBC Show *The Profit*, can go into ANY business and work to turn it around.

There are five platforms in both sports and business you should understand as you use this book as your coach.

1. **You need a PLACE**—This place can be physical, metaphorical or online but it is a HUB for the commerce or

strategy that you offer to the world. It is a sacred place for you and your teams or you and your customers. We have built our place into "The Greatness Factory," a place where we manufacture greatness, and our ultimate goal is to have these in cities around the world. It is a stimulating place where you go when you make a decision to become GREAT in your life. Where's your place going to be?

2. **You need a PROGRAM**—As a coach I had all kinds of programs, including "Life after Basketball," daily success academies, and mentor and leadership programs, to increase the trust, chemistry and competitive intelligence of my players. Now, I have two signature programs in "Monster Producer" and "Turn Your Managers into Coaches," which address problems that we believe we are uniquely qualified to solve. You do not need 30 programs; you just need a few solid ones that play to your core beliefs. Your programs need to solve real problems and be specific and focused.

3. **You need a PRODUCT**—Service businesses succeed when they can deliver sustainable and profitable products without reinventing them every year. (For seven years, I've been trying to find that one product that we can sell off the shelf) In the sports arena, your results are the products; the coaches are vital but you still need a PRODUCT that people cannot live without. Don't build a business around disposable products. Think of building a product that people "have to have" vs "would like to have."

4. **You need a PROCESS**—98% of people don't have a system. They don't have a growth system. They don't

have a selling system. They don't have a marketing system. They don't have an offensive or a game-day system. Once you have the right process in place, you can use it repeatedly; people can be filtered in and out of it even when there is turnover. Start thinking of building something that is teachable, repeatable, scalable, and sellable, whether you're there or not. Read Built to Sell by John Warrilow, which will change the way you build out your business.

5. **You need PEOPLE**—Nothing is scalable without the buy-in and support of the RIGHT PEOPLE. Employees, staff, and teams will always create headaches, but you will never be able to expand if these people don't buy into your vision. If you're a great coach, you must always be recruiting and attracting, coaching and developing, and retaining great talent. Build a team around your unique talents or build a team that can function without you.

I developed the five P concept from my efforts to combine business and sports into a scalable model for my business that can affect more people without being depending on one person. When one person is involved with all of the work, he or she typically goes through a vicious cycle that looks like this:

▶ The person starts with **rejuvenation** and **passion**. The individual loves what he does and gets energy from doing it.

▶ This quickly leads to a **mechanical mode of fatigue, irritability, and agitation** due to the stress of the success he has created for himself and his company.

The individuals burn out because they have spent prolonged periods churning their engine in mechanical mode. They seek outlets that are sometimes destructive, or completely disengage from the efforts and activities that actually led to their initial success. This cycle repeats itself over and over, leaving people tired, overwhelmed, frustrated, and feeling that they can never get ahead. On the other hand, the Coach-epreneur is constantly looking for ways to scale the business into processes and systems that yield profits when he or she is not there. To do this, you need to evaluate the current state of your business. Among the considerations:

1. Do you have a leadership team that can run the business without you?
2. Do you have a sales team that can sell the products or services without you?
3. Do you have a monthly recurring revenue model that is consistent and systematic?
4. Do you have a product that can be sold off the shelf or a heavy service business that requires lots of operations and customer service?
5. How much is your company or idea really worth without your involvement?

When I read the Bible passage on the following page, I thought Jethro was speaking directly to me instead of Moses. I bet in your life you have felt the need to:

- ▶ Control everything.
- ▶ Not delegate because you don't trust your employees or don't have a process in place.
- ▶ Burn the candle at both ends to ensure things get done.

In the Bible, Exodus 18:17–23, there is a marvelous story of scalability with Jethro and Moses that applies to the business world.

One day, as Moses and the Israelites were camping in the wilderness, Jethro came to visit. He took a look at the approach Moses was using to pastor and gave him a better plan to reach the masses, not wear Moses out, and keep everyone fresh and vibrant.

[17]Moses' father-in-law said to him, "What you are doing is not good. [18]You and the people with you will certainly wear yourselves out, for the thing is too heavy for you. You are not able to do it alone. [19]Now obey my voice; I will give you advice, and God be with you! You shall represent the people before God and bring their cases to God, [20]and you shall warn them about the statutes and the laws, and make them know the way in which they must walk and what they must do. [21]Moreover, look for able men from all the people, men who fear God, who are trustworthy and hate a bribe, and place such men over the people as chiefs of thousands, of hundreds, of fifties, and of tens. [22]And let them judge the people at all times. Every great matter they shall bring to you, but any small matter they shall decide themselves. So it will be easier for you, and they will bear the burden with you. [23]If you do this, God will direct you, you will be able to endure, and all these people also will go to their place in peace."

- ▶ Micromanage the process.
- ▶ Work seven days per week and end up burned out and frustrated.

What the Coach-epreneur knows is that this work model is not scalable. In the passage, Jethro explains that this will not only exhaust the leader but the people as well, as they "stand in line" all day waiting to share their story. Does this sound like your customers who are "standing in line" for an answer they believe only you have? This scenario is a set-up for failure. To scale a company you need to step back and think of the end goal and work backwards. You need to create what top lifestyle entrepreneur Scott Nagy calls a "central nervous system" that can respond without you.

When I was coaching teams, in my later career, the smartest move I made was to hire an able-minded and talented "associate head coach" named Tisha Hayes. Tisha was savvy, tough, and didn't take anything from anyone. When I wasn't happy with the direction of my squad or the staff, I simply told her, and she took care of it. This eliminated the NOISE from my life and allowed me to focus on my key priorities. Remember, behind every great #1 is a great #2. In the athletic world, a team's staff consists of a head coach and several assistant coaches but there is typically an associate head coach, the true #2. This person is essentially capable of running the entire organization and may only lack some of the years of experience the head coach has. In the business world you also need a great #2, a second in command. This person has one job: to make the noise go away and free the #1 to do what he or she does best.

A great #2 should:

1. Anticipate the needs of the #1 before he or she shows up.
2. Find out what keeps the #1 up at night and take that pressure away.
3. Clear the path and protect the energy of the #1 so the person can play in his strength zone.
4. Over communicate on "open files" with the #1 to build high trust and execution around ideas.

5. Always take the initiative and not wait until asked to solve problems.
6. Create energy, not subtract it.
7. Be two steps ahead, not two steps behind.

Without a great #2, you are just like Moses trying to teach everyone, listening to every person's challenges, solving all the problems, and expending all of your energy. The Coach-epreneur is part coach and part entrepreneur, so he has an ability to look at a business and find the immediate flaws in the business model. He can see where and why it is not sustainable. Typically, this is because:

- You don't have a clear advantage over your competitors
- Your product or service can quickly become obsolete
- You are the product and the service, leaving room for major missing structures or no scalability
- You are easily "creatively destroyed" by others who can do it better, faster, and cheaper than you.
- You don't have the necessary management team, sales force, marketing arm, or recurring revenue to scale.

The Coach-epreneur Practices Vuja De, Not Déjà Vu

We've talked about the unique perspective on time, energy, resources, and creativity a Coach-epreneur can bring. I also believe a Coach-epreneur practices vuja de versus déjà vu. What is vuja de, you say? Well, let's look at what déjà vu is:

When we encounter something new, but we feel as if we've seen or lived through it before.

The opposite of this would be vuja de, which is when we face something we feel is familiar but we have the ability to see it with a fresh set of eyes. This enables us to offer new insights into old existing problems. It affords us the ability to "extract" our past experiences and immediately apply them to old frames in new ways. The Coach-epreneur rejects the default, becomes a challenger, and pushes back on old norms. For more on being original and understanding how to break old mental models read Adam Grant's book *Originals: How Non-Conformists Move the World*.

What made me a Coach-epreneur early in my career as a head women's basketball coach was that I often extracted business ideas and brought them to the athletic world to give my teams a competitive intelligence. Most coaches were quoting the same old and tired leadership literature, recycling and regenerating ideas from the coaching clinics and attendees year after year. On the other hand, the business concepts were always evolving because of the rapidly changing competitive business landscape. I saw myself as the CEO of a vibrant organization, not just a high school basketball coach. I was looking for a new way to see an old problem.

When I transitioned to the business world, I could see the apathy, boredom, and fatigue in the boardroom. They needed the fire and intensity of a great coach who could bring systems and structure to their workplace and the accountability and discipline that only a championship coach can bring. You can't experience vuja de if you get all your information by going to the same meetings, reading the same books, and spending time with the same people year after year.

Vuja de explains why one coach who has fresh and unique perspective can come into a losing program and turn it around in a very short period. After decades of losing seasons at Alabama, Coach Nick Saban came to the school and within just a few short years, had built a culture of expectation and success by winning national championship after national championship. Jim Harbaugh returned to his alma mater, the University of Michigan, which had years of subpar performance. Harbaugh created energy and enthusiasm quickly for those who desperately needed it. Phil Jackson walked into both the Chicago Bulls and Los Angeles Lakers, took the same players, and won championships when his predecessors could not. All these coaches understand that they can take lower-level resources, including human capital, and convert them into people and systems expecting to win. All these coaches, in very short timespans, change the energy. All these coaches understand and combine business and sports. For instance:

- ▶ Nick Saban's presence is usually enough to convince people to join him at Alabama. His reputational capital precedes him and he is always the buyer, not the seller.

- ▶ Jim Harbaugh understands that business and recruiting are about getting and keeping people's attention, which is why his most recent national signing day included Michigan legend Tom Brady, very much not a Michigan legend Lou Holtz, baseball legend who was a Michigan recruit but did not play there, Derek Jeter (who bypassed Ann Arbor when he was drafted by the New York Yankees, his favorite team), the rapper Migos, pro wrestling legend Ric Flair, NASCAR driver Brad Keselowski, actress Jessica Szohr, ex-Detroit Tigers manager Jim Leyland, and one of the two Sklar brothers. There were also video appearances from actors James Earl Jones, Owen Wilson and Vince Vaughn, NFL legends Mike Ditka and Drew Brees, wrestling legend Bret Hart, former Detroit Pistons coach and noted college basketball analyst Dick Vitale, and many others.

▶ Phil Jackson taught Zen, meditation, and mindfulness to players as a way to calm their thoughts and take them to higher levels of awareness.

Do you see how these coaches brought fresh perspectives to old and tired programs and revived them? When you build something that is alive, vibrant, and attractive, people will be knocking down the door to get in. When you allow something to stagnant, grow boring, disengaged people will be knocking down the door to get out. A Coach-epreneur sees the complete picture, and understands how to create something special, package and sell that special to build tremendous national attention for that creation.

Q AND A WITH COACH BURT

Q: I have been an athletic coach for many years and understand what you are saying but am having a hard time with the business side of this equation. How do I learn this?

A: I constantly studied events and trends in the business world. I would then bring these concepts over to the athletic world and share them with my team in language they could understand. This sharpened both their skills and my skills and built what I called a "competitive intelligence." My players were smarter than players on other teams, which gave us an intangible advantage. Most coaches don't understand this and only compete in the game. What happens when you meet people more capable than you? How do you win? I believe you can sometimes outwork people but if all things are equal, you may be able to outsmart them. The body is where talent is. I wanted to work on the mind, the heart, and the spirit. Very few coaches understand the breadth and depth of these dimensions. You can buy a man's hand but you cannot buy his heart. He either freely gives it to you or he distances it from you. To play at the highest levels you have to become a "master of human potential."

Q: I believe I need a good #2. What attributes should the person have?

A: Behind every great #1 is a great #2. First, the person must be 100% loyal to your vision. The individual should take care of as many tasks as possible to free you up to do what you do best. The skill set of a #2 should complement, not compete with yours. They must always have your back and be comfortable in a support role. Some #2s start to believe they can be the #1 and become jealous of your skill sets or the rewards you get. They simply don't yet have the skills to be a #1 but may mature into one in the future.

Q: My organization is stale and needs a breath of fresh air. What do you suggest?

A: Your brain is wired to get bored very easily. What you need is fresh, dynamic, and progressive ideas. Without these kinds of ideas, your organization becomes stale and complacent. Your job as the leader is to mix up the energy. You may need to bring in someone new. You may need to change locations. You can't allow yourself or anyone in your shop to become complacent. I travel a lot. This requires me to step out of my day-to-day routine and look at life from fresh and interesting perspectives. This is how I do not let myself get stale. I go to various regions of the country and world and study what others are doing.

6

ACTIVATING YOUR INTANGIBLE SUCCESS FACTORS

Have you ever tried to figure out how someone inferior in talent can beat someone very talented? After all, doesn't talent always win? Nope, sometimes David really does beat Goliath. The underdogs win from time to time and they can rise to the top. They can do this because of something I call an "intangible." The great coach Don Meyer of David Lipscomb University always said, "I'm looking for people who are an A in talent and an A in mindset" but if they do not have both, I'm not interested in an A in talent and a B in mindset. I'll take a B in talent any day with an A in mindset over a kid that has talent but no drive." That "drive," that "hustle," that "underdog spirit," and that belief" is precisely what we are going to explain in this chapter.

Intangibles cannot be measured which is why they don't get the credit they deserve. On a profit and loss statement, you will never see something you cannot touch, but it is most certainly there. It is often the intangibles that cost your team forward momentum, the bounce back you need to break through and get up when you're knocked down, or the trust that serves as the glue, which holds you together during crisis. ***An intangible is like a hidden asset.*** It is there whether you want to admit it or not. Most of my life I've been able to win on the intangibles. An intangible could be any of the following:

▸ Trust
▸ Chemistry
▸ Knowledge
▸ Expertise
▸ Grit

▸ Focus
▸ Bounce back/Resilience
▸ Likeability
▸ Buy-in
▸ Faith

There are more words I could include but this list shows you why intangibles are so essential to success. Let us revisit the "Whole Person Theory" (from chapter 2) for an illustration to see where the intangibles fit in:

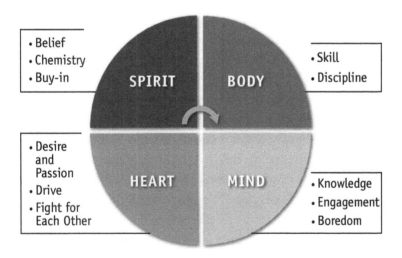

Often, when I spoke at the Final Four conference, I would ask coaches, "When you lost last year how many of you lost because you didn't practice enough?" I knew the answer so it was really a trick question. I knew they all practiced their players as much as the NCAA would allow. The next questions were, "How many of you lost because your team was just less talented than other teams in your conference?" This too was a trick query because many in the room were in charge of recruiting those duds. Once we got past those two questions, we then got in to the real problem.

"How many of you lost because of one of these reasons?"

1. Trust between you and the team and the players in each other.
2. Chemistry between you and the players and between them.
3. Toughness or bounce back.
4. Buy-in to you, the system, or each other.
5. Knowledge of the game and your systems.
6. Faith in you or what you were doing.
7. Grit.
8. Specific basketball IQ, meaning the players didn't have high levels of IQ about how to execute.

Hands around the room would go up until almost everyone had raised theirs. I would then say, "These things have nothing to do with SKILL, which is the BODY; they have everything to do with the 'hidden parts' of a person's nature, meaning the mind, the heart, and the spirit." I would then ask, "How are you coaching these parts?" Very few, if any, had any answers.

In the business world, what good is it to have a salesperson who has knowledge (mind) but doesn't have the work ethic or hustle to work the system (heart)? What good is it to have knowledge (mind) with no confidence (spirit)? That is why simply telling people to work harder or make more phone calls is the equivalent of athletes practicing for more hours. You're not getting to the root of the problem because it is intangible.

Think of a tangible as something you can feel, taste, touch, measure, or see. This is quantitative, which means it can be measured. Think of an intangible as something you can sense, feel, or have an intuition about. This is qualitative and cannot be measured. This is where most games in the business world and on the athletic field are won or lost. My specialty in both business and sports has always been in "activating the intangibles," and this is a skill set that, with some training, you too can activate.

When looking for a competitive intelligence, an inch of separation, you need to understand where that advantage can come from and it may not be in your team's skill sets. The inch of separation is in the collaboration among people who will fight for each other every day. It's in the trust, the chemistry, the knowledge, the energy, and culture of each person. For you to activate these "hidden assets" you need to understand the following:

1. **The body's need is to live.** This is where both skill and discipline come from, and where the need for money meets physical needs. You need to work on disciplines, cultivating self-discipline, and teaching skills daily. You also need to compensate people fairly and give them an opportunity for earning power through performance compensation. Unfortunately, many managers never offer training for their employees but instead leave it up to the staff to "figure it out" by going to a workshop or boot camp or at its worst, just reading a book. However, when you improve your staff's skills, they can perform

at a higher level. Remember, trained people outperform untrained people any day of the week. Keep this saying in the back of your mind: "Contented cows give more milk." Studies show that cows that are given a name produce 6% more milk than those that don't have a name. Pay attention to your cows.

2. **The mind needs to learn, be engaged, and grow.** Once the mind learns, it never goes back to its original dimension. At work, people get bored, especially if they never get a chance to learn. When they're bored, people moonlight, daydream, or check out and end up just collecting a paycheck. You need to focus weekly on engaging your employees by offering new learning strategies, new problems to solve, new areas to explore, and exposure to bigger and bigger thinking. Most organizations never challenge their workforce, which leads to a cold and dull culture. In fact, people want to engage in higher levels of thinking and be challenged. By offering advancement into new and exciting areas, you will maintain an employee population that continues to learn and grow.

3. **The heart's need is to love and be loved.** It craves passion, validation, and affirmation. We've become increasingly inadequate at validating the desires of others. We seldom celebrate success in a consistent and systematic manner. We don't recognize people in front of their peers often enough to validate their contribution or acknowledge the long hours they put into projects and the overall success of the company. Sometimes a simple but genuine "thank you" or "we appreciate you" is all it takes for someone to be aware that their

contribution to the whole has made a difference. We also fail to recognize people's true abilities and place them into the correct role around their core passions. When I placed my VP of sales, Bruce Lund, into a new role in the company creating, teaching, and facilitating a new division called Talent Supply and offered him an incentive based on top line revenue, he took complete ownership of that division. He wakes up daily on fire to produce because we are rewarding his body (financial/ skills), mind (ownership of new ideas), heart (passion), and spirit (faith in him and us). Place people in their areas of strength and see how hard they will work. When people experience a "broken heart" in their life they are likely to "fight or flee." If they fight, they will become vindictive toward the leaders and the company. If they flee they will check out and still show up in the body, but their most important parts—mind, heart, or spirit—will not be there.

4. **The spirit needs to connect to a higher power, to have faith, and to grow confidence.** If your employees don't believe in what you are doing, or have lost "faith" in you, you and your business are in trouble. You constantly need to talk about the vision, mission and purpose of the company, outside of just making money. You need to build a faith-based company where people want to work and be a part of the team. What happens when people lose "faith" in themselves or their employers? They check out or disengage. They seek other work that will fill this need in their lives. I believe SQ (spiritual intelligence) drives all other intelligences, and this is where both conscience and intuition come from.

As you can see, there is more to this equation than just the body. A recent study showed that nearly 67% of Americans said they did just enough not to be fired at work. This is disturbing. What happens to teams when their players do just enough not to be kicked off the team? The teams lose. The players give up and they quit. What happens in marriages when the heart, mind, and spirit are not engaged? Both spouses lose. One person quits, gives up, shows up but is not really there. When you understand how to activate the intangibles in other people, you understand that you MUST connect to all four parts of their nature.

A few other key intangibles either attract or repel people:

- Likeability
- Connectivity
- Deep Networks
- Chemistry
- Bounce back
- Creativity

Today, you sometimes hear that people don't care how likeable you are if you're an expert, but human nature says that if I like you (meaning you bring positive energy) and you are an expert, then you will win out over someone who is unlikeable and an expert. I once coached a financial advisor from Memphis who had all the basic ingredients for success—the knowledge, the skills, the desire, and the confidence. However, he lacked completely in likeability. Nobody wanted to do business with him because of his demeanor. In addition, it was hard to coach him because his lack of likeability came from his mind-set of superiority. He was condescending and he instantly gave off a negative vibe. I look at the spirit of people for signs of:

1. Negativity
2. Scarcity
3. Competitiveness

4. Contention
5. Complacency
6. Cynicism
7. Dissension
8. Animosity
9. Superiority

All of these are intangibles, by the way, and they will all cost you. In addition, there are the intangibles related to dress, image, perception, and brand value you create by how you look, speak, respond, or the people with whom you associate. All of these factors either increase or decrease your value. They can be difficult to articulate so consider these questions:

1. Do you have the spirit of any of the intangible qualities that can hurt you? If you said no, there's another intangible you need to address—pride.
2. Do you believe "outdated clothing equals outdated mind-sets"? If so, it may be time to revisit your wardrobe, appearance, or looks.
3. Does your body say to the world that you take care of yourself or have you let yourself go? Is there a direct correlation between your own self-discipline and your ability to take care of your customers?
4. Do you bring your negative attitude from your past into your present?
5. Do people feel better about themselves or worse when they are with you?
6. Does the car you drive, where you live, or who you associate with increase or decrease your perceived "reputational capital"?

When I ask the question, "If I gave you some hard feedback about your appearance, clothing, brand, or image, would you be willing to change it?" Ninety percent of people say they would but they don't really understand the importance of the intangibles. These are all intangibles because I can't tell you how much money you are losing by wearing torn jeans from the 1980s. I can't tell you how much money you are losing by hanging out with your friends, what you post on Facebook, or even the car you drive. However, what I can tell you is that perception is reality for many; people size up you and your brand in a matter of minutes, if not seconds. If you underestimate the power of these intangibles, then you are underestimating not only the assets that could have the biggest impact on your bottom-line as well the biggest drivers for long-term success and what separates you from your competition.

I made a living by winning on the intangibles. Let me show you how you can win the close ones in life just by excelling in these areas.

How to Build Your "Competitive Intelligence" with Your Team

After listening to hall of fame coach Don Meyer, I made a commitment at age 18 that I would use sports to teach life skills and that work would become the vehicle for my talents. This was the best decision I ever made because the more I helped my players develop as people, the more wins they produced, giving credence to the concept of the "geese laying the golden eggs." I also made the commitment that Covey's *The 7 Habits of Highly Effective People* would be the foundation of the teaching I use with every player. These are habits of effectiveness that carry over into any field or profession.

This began a habit that many coaches to this day still don't get, or won't take the time to understand. It's a trend I call "competitive intelligence." When you are looking for an inch of differentiation for your team in highly competitive or even saturated markets, you need something that separates you. It can be just one point of separation, one sale of separation, or one dollar of separation. I always believed that my advantage was that *my players were smarter than other people's players, my players were more connected emotionally to each other than other people's players, and that my players had a higher team intelligence than other people's players.* Therefore, the question becomes how do you build this "competitive intelligence?"

There are two parts to leadership: the **technical competency and the humanistic side.** The former deals with skill, numbers, and the basics of the job description. Any competent manager or coach can knows this part, or they wouldn't have been elevated to a leadership position. However, **what many don't comprehend is the humanistic side.** This is the part of intelligence that deals with the intangibles of the heart, the mind, and the spirit. These parts directly affect buy-in, leadership, resilience, trust, and commitment—and these qualities, my friend, are responsible for how you win. When coaches and managers don't deal with this "soft side," as many call it, these intangibles won't be part of the teamwork. Lacking an awareness of the humanistic side will cost you in the long run, and will show up at the most inopportune time. If you've been a coach for any period of time, you know exactly what I'm talking about.

I remember many years ago coaching the 15 top players in the state of Tennessee. We were hand-selected, both coaches and players, to play the best teams in the country. There were players from all socioeconomic backgrounds and all skill levels. They were the best of the best with egos and parents to match their skill sets. I proposed that at the beginning of each practice we teach *life, success, leadership, and intangibles* using a series of exercises to build this important humanistic side. After all, the players barely knew each other and we were expecting them to compete and win against really tough opponents. However, one of the other coaches who had an old-school philosophy said, "Nope, let's get them up and start practicing because we don't have them for long and this is a waste of time." I simply said, "There is more to winning than practicing. Here is what I predict will happen. When push comes to shove and the pressure is on, I believe they will bail out on each other. Why in the world would they fight for someone whom they don't even know, understand, or believe in?" And that's exactly what happened. Although we won some games (mostly on talent), when push came to shove we lost because there wasn't a "competitive intelligence" built by the coaches and players, and that was our fault, not theirs.

To understand the differences, consider these factors:

Technical Competency	Humanistic
1. Skill	1. Heart
2. Numbers	2. Trust
3. Tracking	3. Motivation
4. Systems	4. Chemistry
5. Structure	5. Structure
6. Training	6. Training
7. Assembly Work	7. Team Unity
8. Repetitive Nature	8. Leadership

Qualities from both categories are necessary here to win but unlike my approach, many coaches only stress the mechanics. That means there's no fire. There's no passion. There's no spirit.

There's no pull toward the future vision. It's all boring, automated and about competency and skills. Coaching this way leaves the team without the most important ingredients needed for winning.

I wrote the book *The Intangibles* because championship coach and good friend Cory Barrett called me one Saturday afternoon and said, "I want to do all of those things you did with your team to build the intangibles but I don't know what to teach." I said, "If I give you 40 lessons would you teach them daily in a 40-day cycle and elaborate on them?" He said, "Absolutely." That afternoon I sat down by the pool and wrote the book. I would sacrifice competency of practicing to build the inside of a person and the inside of a team. Just as you practice on skills, you need to practice on inner engineering your team to fight the real battle, which is between the ears, and in the heart and spirit. If a coach doesn't help you build this "competitive intelligence," then you're left to compete solely on your athletic ability. In addition, when you meet people who are better athletes, you're screwed, as is your coach. You don't have any tools left in your tool shed, leaving talent and skill versus talent and skill. There will always be someone who is bigger, faster, and stronger.

You're my coach. Grow my whole person. Activate my intangibles. Inner engineer me to win from the inside out. Work DAILY on both the technical side of winning and the humanistic side of winning and watch how hard I will fight for both you and my teammates. This will get you the wins when all talent is equal or your talent is disproportionate to your competition in the boardroom or in the locker room.

Q AND A WITH COACH BURT

Q: I'm a coach and see the need for the "intangibles" but don't know how to activate them in my unit. What do I do?

A: This is a common challenge for most coaches. You can't teach or activate intangibles until you understand "The Whole Person Theory." Briefly, here is what you need to do:

    a. Activate the body in this way: Constantly grow the skill level of your staff on a weekly basis. In sports, this is easy. You work on conditioning and actual skills. In corporate America, offer coaching on the actual work they do. Sharpen their skill sets and help them "skill up."

    b. Activate the mind this way: Constantly engage them in new ways to stimulate their minds. Give them different tasks. Challenge them. Put them in positions to learn. Never allow them to grow bored or tired from doing monotonous work.

    c. Activate the heart this way: Value them. Appreciate them. Honor their contribution. Celebrate with them. Stoke their passion, do not squelch it.

    d. Activate the spirit this way: Talk about vision and where the company is going and their role in it. Use work as a vehicle to do good in the world. Help them retain their faith in you and the purpose of the company. Show them the fruits of their labor.

Q: My team has checked out on me with the heart. What do I do?

A: I've lost teams who shut down on me. This could be related to a lack of passion on their part (you may have the wrong people) or because they feel like you have "broken their hearts." This means they constantly give their all-out effort for you only they think you crush their spirt. You may need to re-evaluate your stance and your heart or you may need to clean house and find people who believe the same things you do.

Q: I've noticed that chemistry is lacking in my unit. I have good players but they just don't play together. How can I solve this?

A: Chemistry is a function of two people wanting the same thing. It is a function of personality and shared values. My goal with all of my teams was to unite them around one dominant focus and to force them to spend time with each other. We learn to respect each other when we struggle together. I put my team through all kinds of artificial adversity to speed up the maturation process and I would not bail them out. They had to "work their way out of binds" by relying on each other. This helps build their chemistry. I also put them in various social structures outside of the game to help them bond, get to know each other better, and believe in each other.

7

BUILDING A TEAM IN A "FREE AGENT NATION"

I remember it like it was yesterday. I was sitting in a locker room in Smyrna, Tennessee, dejected, lonely, and frustrated. My team had just shut down on me completely. Well, not my whole team, just everyone except my best player Anne Marie Lanning. The rest of the squad was on one team, and Anne Marie and I were on the other. They had turned against us. They had given up and now it was a war of selfish proportion. I knew if I did not get them back over to my side and my way of thinking, it was going to be a long and miserable year. This team, like any selfish team that lacked all the important ingredients, was going to be under-performing, going home early, and then doing what they did best, which was blame it on everybody else. I had a "free agent nation" on my hands.

A "free agent nation" represents a country where everyone's mindset is about "What's in it for me?" This attitude of entitlement permeates our society and starts at an early age and then spills over into later in life when potential hires lead with this question in a job interview, "How many days do I get off and what is included in my benefits package?" Try building a championship culture with teams that have this mindset.

Paradigm was a word I learned at age 18. I didn't know what it meant at the time but later understood it meant "the individual lens in which you see the world." It is affected by all your thoughts, every conversation you have, every bias you acquired while growing up, every TV show you watch, and every book you read. *It is UNIQUE to you.* While in college pursuing my doctorate degree I took a class in "bias, assumption, and prejudice." Why did I have to take this class, I wondered, and what does it have to do with leadership and teams? *It turns out that it has everything to do with leadership and teams.* We all bring our own bias, assumption, and prejudice to EVERY encounter with another person. This includes years of personal and emotional baggage and dysfunction because we are inherently dysfunctional people. We are imperfect people who live in an imperfect world. When we bring our "paradigm" into an encounter with someone or a group of people, we are essentially "colliding" our thought processes with theirs. Even Oren Klaff in *Pitch Anything: An Innovative Method for Presenting, Persuading and Winning the Deal* noted that there is always a "collision of frames" and somebody wins and somebody loses. I go for win-win or no deal when I enter but the reality is it doesn't always turn out that way. When we place people in teams without providing proper management and coaching, we "compound" the dysfunction because we are bringing together varying viewpoints and trying to make them unite. This collision can create frustration, exhaustion, and drastic underperformance.

This is why a good coach is vital. The coach is helping to "sell" one vision, one paradigm, and one concept to the group. Coaches who are poor at "managing this energy" end up with a "free agent nation" of lone wolf bandits and self-centered players who never perform at the highest levels. This will destroy the team as people move in all different directions, have low levels of productivity, and is usually accompanied by the seven emotional cancers. These "cancers" include:

- Comparing
- Complaining
- Contending
- Criticizing
- Complacency
- Cynicism
- Competing

A cancer is a differentiated cell in the body that loses its social identity within the group and then attacks the "healthy cells" it needs to live and survive. Within teams, this usually begins with one person separating himself from the group and then persuading others to join him and his "point of view" (paradigm), where they secretly plot to destroy or undermine the group. These people are referred to as "emotional cancers" and they eat away at the good will and energy of the entire group. This self-sabotaging from the inside causes disharmony, resentment, and bitterness; it consumes an enormous amount of energy that you need to use in the real battle, in the marketplace and against your competitors.

This is why every leader is in sales. He is selling his vision. He is selling his ideas. He is selling harmony. He is selling success. He is selling potential. If he fails to sell this ONE vision, he ends up with many fragmented visions. A team that does not share how they see the world will show all signs of the *Five Dysfunctions of Teams* that Patrick Lencioni writes about including:

- *Absence of trust*—The emotional bank account is low between two parties and there is no vulnerability with each other, only judgment.

- ▸ *Fear of conflict*—The leader and group will not address unmet expectations, leading to artificial harmony and underperformance.
- ▸ *Avoidance of accountability*—People can do whatever they want, whenever they want, with little or no accountability.
- ▸ *Lack of commitment*—Some are more committed than others which breeds resentment.
- ▸ *Status and ego*—Typically, this is where the most talented people in the group show their selfishness by believing they are above the rules of the group and are free to choose as they please. This too breeds enormous amounts of resentment toward the others.

Lencioni had it right: teams are dysfunctional. However, I think are way more than five dysfunctions. Sometimes, teams can have many more because of extreme selfishness in today's world. This is why it is so hard to build effective teams, because ultimately, it all comes down to what one person believes versus another.

To combat these dysfunctions, I spent an enormous amount of time as a coach educating the "conscience" of my players. A conscience is an internal voice that prompts people to take certain actions in alignment with what is right and wrong. However, sometimes, people have never had their conscience educated correctly. Were some of your team members not taught the difference between right and wrong when they were young? That's right; I had players who stole from each other and called it "borrowing" because that's what they did in their house. When they didn't have an item, they just took it from someone else. As a coach and leader, you will often have to educate and correct the conscience of your team. This is why so many coaches and leaders struggle. It takes an enormous amount of time and energy to constantly rebuke your team members when they don't adhere to the core principles and vision you have outlined or too which they have committed.

How can you educate the conscience of your team? Here are some strategies that I used:

1. We taught all players the "7 Habits of Highly Effective People" the minute they came into our program.

2. We taught "The Five Dysfunctions of Teams" to the point that the individuals could police each other and correct each other when they were practicing these dysfunctions.

3. We had daily success and leadership academies with capable potential leaders to build internal leadership.

4. We focused our meetings on both technical competency (50%) and the humanistic side of leadership for conscience building (50%).

5. We spent just as much time on the heart, the mind, and the spirit as we did on the body or skill.

6. We gave our players the ability to "throw the red flag," which is a concept Jim Collins discusses in *Good to Great: Why Some Companies Make the Leap...And Others Don't*, where anyone in the organization can call a foul on another person if something the individual is doing will mitigate the end goal.

7. We taught each person the "Whole Person" theory so it was easy to diagnose, prescribe, and predict where someone needed work.

All these strategies were geared at educating the conscience of every team member. When players were misaligned, there were consequences because "where there is no consequence there is no change of behavior." Let me say that again so it sticks with you, as this relates to both children and adults: "Where there are no consequences there is no change of behavior." If team members can simply do whatever they want whenever they want, then why would they change? I also believe that "satisfied needs never motivate people, only unsatisfied needs." The reason so many become complacent is because their needs are met and they don't desire for more.

All of this plays into why it is so dang hard to build a team. We've got misaligned paradigms, bias and assumption, and faulty a team conscience. If you then add in no consequences to behavior that is counterproductive to the team vision or satisfied needs, then you end up with one big mess. It all starts with who you recruit and attract, which is where core values versus shared values comes into play.

Core Values Versus Shared Values

When most people talk about core values, they're boring. They say things like trust, honesty, integrity, and team work. Blah, blah, blah. In my mind, these should be givens. We shouldn't have to stress that we should be trustworthy, kind to the customers and to each other, and work with integrity. I want to change the way you see core values and explain that the real problem in any relationship stems from the differences or misalignment in what you see (the paradigm), and what you believe (core values).

A core value is "something you believe in your core." For example, I believe:

- ▶ Work should be the distribution channel for your talents.
- ▶ We should come in early and stay until the job is finished.
- ▶ All my responsibilities should be in my job description.
- ▶ We don't whine, we don't complain, and we don't make excuses.
- ▶ Sales are that lifeblood of every company, and revenue is king.
- ▶ A good operations team can be a company's real competitive advantage.
- ▶ A person should always start out on the operations side to truly learn and understand the business.
- ▶ We have 365 days per year and we get to choose what we do with them.

These are all things that I believe at my core. They are part of my "core values." Now, let's say that I hire or recruit you but you believe the exact opposite of what I believe. How long do you think it would take before we had a problem with each other?

We should do business with people who believe the same things we do.

We should hire and recruit people who believe the same things we do.

We should partner and form strategic alliances with people who believe the same things we do.

We should part ways with employees in our companies who don't share our core values.

Nevertheless, there is a caveat: Just because I believe something at my core doesn't make it right. Therefore, if I choose to only hire people who believe the same things I do because it's my company, that's my prerogative. Steve Jobs believed in challenging the status quo in everything Apple did. He also believed that "A" players didn't want to play with "B" players; therefore, he only surrounded himself with other people who wanted the same things he did and believed the same things he did.

When I have to let an employee go, I simply say, "I place a high value on this and you don't seem to place that same value on it. This doesn't make me right and you wrong or you right and me wrong. We simply are not on the same page about what we believe, and because of that, we need to part ways."

I don't think you always have to agree on politics or religion. You don't have to line up on what how you spend your free time or what are your favorite restaurants are, but you do need to match up on major issues. When I draw up "Core Values versus Shared Values" it typically looks like this:

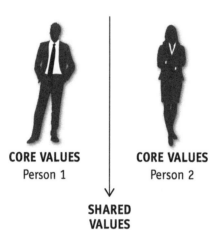

CORE VALUES
Person 1

CORE VALUES
Person 2

**SHARED
VALUES**

If the core values of person #1 don't line up with the shared values of person #2, then misalignment of values happens. Watch what happens next...

The Commitment Continuum

Have you ever seen a team that was losing and watched the players' body language? You can sense their lack of belief and commitment to each other and their vision. Their body language says that there is little or no faith in each other and their bigger future. They slump over. They pout. They whine and complain. Many times, they end up fighting or arguing. This is the manifestation of two or more people who don't share core values. They don't want the same things. They either rebel or quit, maliciously obey, or practice willing compliance.

Now, let's contrast this with a team of people who are on FIRE for each other. They will fight for each other. They will claw for each other. They will push to the end for each other. Their energy is contagious and you want to cheer for them because they are so aligned with each other and the shared vision. They bring creative excitement. They bring heartfelt commitment. They bring high levels of energy and synergy. This is the manifestation of a group of people who share core values. They believe in the same things and want the exact same things. This is illustrated in "The Commitment Continuum" originally created by Dr. Stephen Covey.

Rebel or Quit	Malicious Obedience	Willing Compliance	Heartfelt Commitment	Creative Excitement

Now, let's break these down so you can see and sense where you and your team are on the continuum.

1. Rebel or quit—Is it possible for people to show up "in the body" every day but not be there in the mind, heart,

and spirit? Of course, they can. Two people can be in a relationship with each other but have quit on each other. You can rebel against authority, the system, or the culture.

2. *Malicious obedience*—This means you say one thing to a person's face and another behind his back. You obey but you do so in such a way that it builds an undercurrent of resistance underneath the surface. Common terms for this are undermining or backstabbing.

3. *Willing compliance*—There is a big difference between being committed and being obligated. Willing compliance represents people who show up every day and just "go through the motions" for each other. These people are "obligated," meaning their heart is not present. I challenge you on this. Name one thing in your life that you've been great at that in which your heart was not included? I bet you'll find it hard to name something.

4. *Heartfelt commitment*—This is where you are IN with your whole self. You are totally committed to seeing something through to its logical conclusion. You are willing to do the inconvenient it takes to be successful.

5. *Creative excitement*—This is where you bring energy and ideas to the equation. You bring your spirit of creativity and your passion to solve problems, add value, and play at the highest levels of production. This goes beyond just showing up and doing the deal. You are bringing the "intangibles" of mind, heart, and spirit to the party.

Now, what does this look like? Levels one, two, and three are bad or mediocre teams. Levels four and five are championship teams. This is where all of your commitment comes from. It comes from lining up on what you believe at your core, in your soul, and with your heart. It begins by having "shared values."

- ▶ When you recruit, you need to recruit to shared values.
- ▶ When you build your team, build it to shared values.
- ▶ When you get rid of people, get rid of them because they violate the shared values.

Trust me; this is where great teams start and how they win at the highest levels. They believe and want the same things, and when you believe and want the same things, you begin to "make the noise go away" for each other. You begin to remove all "emotional tax" on the people around you.

The Emotional Tax

Bad teams tax all the players (and the coach) emotionally. They wear on each other. Trust is low. Follow-through is poor and the Emotional Bank Account is empty or bankrupt. An "Emotional Tax" is something that is levied on a person typically by an outside party or force that steals future momentum or profits. This tax does not cost you money, although it certainly could, but it costs you the intangibles. It costs you:

- ▶ Time
- ▶ Energy
- ▶ Chemistry
- ▶ Trust
- ▶ Future profits
- ▶ Enjoyment
- ▶ Joy
- ▶ Passion

Some of the greatest emotional taxes in the world come at the expense of those in the same office with us. Sometimes they come from a spouse who beats you up when you go home because he or she isn't supportive of your dreams, so the person make small digs toward you in subtle ways. An emotional tax could come in the form of a passive-aggressive co-worker who misdirects his unhappiness with life or his inability to perform on you. Regardless of where the "Emotional Tax" comes from, it wears on you and takes away much of the forward momentum you need to produce. It steals your joy and thunder. It taxes you emotionally to the point that you constantly are frustrated, irritated, and exhausted.

Once you understand how taxing this can be, you realize that we should be protecting each other from this "tax." We should be building, maintaining, and protecting each other's confidence, not destroying it. However, some people thrive on the drama of office politics and this emotional burden.

Ask yourself, "How much emotional tax is going on right now in your office and how long are you going to tolerate it?" Remember that we encourage what we allow.

Now do you see why it is so hard to build a team? All these factors and variables are fighting against the unity of a group. All these factors, combined with a "free agent" nation and an entitlement mind-set, are eroding a great team. A great team should be composed of trusting people who have strong chemistry, no emotional taxes, and share vulnerability with each other.

Q AND A WITH COACH BURT

Q: My team is a "free agent nation." What do I do?

A: This is a function of one thing: a lack of shared values. If you can recruit, I would tell you to get very clear about your core values and only recruit people who believe the same things. Go the distance in the interview process to be sure that everyone lines up. When you don't line up you get "rebelling or quitting," malicious obedience, or willing compliance. If you cannot recruit and are stuck with this group of duds, you better dig in and start selling. Sell them on how these core values will help them. Constantly educate the heart, mind, and conscience on why team dysfunctions will destroy what you could produce together. This is a sales job for the leader and you need to start selling this every week.

Q: How do we avoid placing "The Emotional Tax" on one another?

A: That's a great question. An emotional tax is a levy typically placed on one's future potential and created by other people bytheir lack of preparation, low wasted and negative energy and drama, and overall poor attitude and disposition. Confront the emotional taxers and either shape them up or ship them out. I don't tolerate people who drag everybody else down with their attitude and mindset. Either you fit or you don't and and emotional tax inevitably spreads to others.

Q: My team lacks the intangible of chemistry. They are all talented but can't seem to connect?

A: Remember when I told you about the old school coach who only wanted the top performers to practice but didn't want them to connect emotionally? I'm a big believer in spending time on the front end and throughout the experience together bonding, building chemisty, and getting lost in each other's dreams. As an athletic coach I spent more than five hours per day with my players. This builds chemistry. We connected. We shared struggles together. We won together. We lost together. We laughed together. We cried toghether. We may not always like each other but we have to build a respect around the core vision of where we're headed. I put my teams together outside of the game so players could bond and connect with each other. They could share and dig in. I also placed an enormous amount of artificial adversity on them so they had to communicate and work together to get the ball across the finish line.

RUNNING THROUGH
A WALL FOR YOUR COACH

Think back to someone who communicated and validated your worth and potential so clearly that you begin to believe it in your own self. Think back to how that person saw the good in you when it was easy to see the bad. Think about the enormous growth you experienced in your life because of that person. Think of how that relationship was transformational vs. transactional. Think of the loyalty and respect you feel for that person. Think of how that one person changed your life. Now imagine for one second that this person asks you do to something for him or her. I bet you don't say, "Well, I just don't have time," or "I wish I could." I bet you say, "I would do anything for you." I would run through the wall for you.

I very seldom, if ever, hear a person say, "I would run through the wall for my manager." Nevertheless, I do hear individuals say, "I would run through the wall for my coach." **Many see their manager or boss as an adversary**. Employees and managers are often fighting and are "against" rather than "for" each other. As a coach, you want to mitigate this type of thinking. You want to understand that your workers and your players are the "geese laying the golden eggs." If you have never understood or heard the story of Aesop, it goes like this:

> *Aesop had a goose that laid golden eggs. He could take those eggs into town and sell them, making him very wealthy. It was the goose that was producing Aesop's wealth. The problem came when Aesop got greedy and believed that if he just killed the goose that she would have more golden eggs inside her. Greed is an intense and selfish desire for something, especially wealth, power, or food. In this case, Aesop's greed was for wealth and this greed prompted him to take poor actions, resulting in the loss of his future profits. He taxed himself with his actions.*

As a coach and leader, your people, both internally and externally, are your geese. They are producing the golden eggs for you. They are the ones giving you both production and more production capacity. As a solo-preneur or single leader without followers, you don't have any production capacity. You only have limited production. To grow or scale you will have to entrust others and work on meeting their needs so they will WANT to produce more for you. *Remember this: people do not leave their jobs; they leave their bosses.* You want your people fighting for you. You want your people on fire for you. You want your people producing at the highest levels possible. How then do we become coaches for whom people would run through the wall? We create unique value through our knowledge, skills, desire, and confidence, which we share, with our team in a consistent and systematic manner. It's what we constantly pour into our people.

We know that "content cows" give more milk, so we extract and share with our people on a daily, weekly, and monthly basis so they know that we care about their whole self, their body, their mind, their heart, and their spirit. They know that we want to meet their needs in big ways, and this builds a bond and a loyalty to us and the vision that we need to prosper. This is where ALL of your production capacity comes from.

This relationship cannot be adversarial. This relationship cannot be competitive. This relationship has to be fruitful for "both" parties, so look at it this way. Many people bring me in as a coach to get "more" out of their current people. They want me to squeeze, push, cajole, motivate through fear, and somehow motivate them to produce in higher and higher ways. For years, I did it this way, with a two-by-four. However, this is only a short- term fix to a long- term problem. This only works when the external force or motivator is present. The minute the external force is no longer there, the motivation dissipates. We need something that is sustainable. We need something that sticks. We need something that is not cotton candy. Instead of asking, "How do we get more out of our people?" let us ask, "How do we meet our people's core needs so they will give us more?"

Core needs are:

- ▸ The body's need is to live.
- ▸ The mind's need is to learn.
- ▸ The heart's need is to love.
- ▸ The spirit's need is to leave a legacy, connect to a higher source, and make a mark on the world.

If work could become the distribution channel for someone's talent, then how do we make work a place that taps into all four parts of a person's nature? How do we tap into the "whole goose," which would mean the geese would lay more golden eggs for the cause? How do we make our work our own little "Greatness Factory"? One thing is for certain, if we destroy the very thing that is producing our bigger futures, then we cannot expect our prosperity or wealth to grow. We will never be scalable. We will always be limited.

Early on in my coaching career, I led through fear. I led through consequence. I led through breaking people's spirits—and this did work, *to a point*. I never won a championship during this tenure of my career as I was "killing" the very thing that produced my wealth. I was killing the geese that laid the golden eggs. Let us revisit the essential question you should be asking. It is not, "How do I squeeze more out of the people I've got?" Instead, ask, "How do I meet my people's core needs so they will give me more?"

Here are my strategies for producing "contented cows" who give more milk:

1. Tap into their body by growing their skills on a consistent basis and meeting their financial needs with incentives for performance.
2. Tap into their mind by engaging them with new and exciting work, allowing them to work in areas in which they're interested and give them constant chances to learn at work.
3. Tap into their heart by validating their success with affirmation, success rallies, and noting their work ethic and contribution to the overall whole.
4. Tap into their spirit by bringing your faith to work and letting them know of your deep convictions.
5. Offer them a chance to share in that faith. Talk vision. Talk strategy. Talk expansion and growth. Also, talk legacy, meaning, and contribution.

One of the best strategies I ever used as a head coach was to walk with various players after practice down at the football field. It became famous as "the walk" and players joked with each other wondering, "When is Coach Burt going to take you on that walk?" I would simply signal to a player to stick around after practice because I wanted to take a stroll with that person. On that walk, we focused on one thing: what I could do to be a better leader and coach for the player. We focused on the player's needs, fears, and anxieties. We focused on having meaningful conversation. I was feeding my sheep and tending to my lambs. You cannot imagine how this one conversation drove up our retention rate and ability to fight for each other because there was real meat on the bone. It did wonders for our relationships. We need to get back to these types of conversations. We need to "slow down" to "speed up." We need to do a better job of feeding our sheep.

While at a marriage conference called XQ in South Lake, Texas, at Gateway Church, one of the fastest growing churches in the country, I became curious. When I get curious I go looking for answers and ways to "extract" and "synthesize information" to make it useful to those I serve. I wanted to know how this church, founded in 2000 with just 167 people in attendance, now had an attendance of 36,000 strong just 16 years later. On the break, I wondered into the bookstore. I stumbled upon Pastor Robert Morris' book *The Blessed Church: The Simple Secret to Growing the Church You Love*. The book outlines his "growth strategy" and discusses the power of meeting your people's core needs and how healthy, well-fed sheep grow and multiply. They "fight for the cause to expand and multiply."

His secret could be found by studying the 21st chapter of John, where Jesus has three conversations with Peter after the death and resurrection and asks him, "Do you love me?" Peter, all three times, says, "Yes Lord, you know I love you." Three times Jesus asking signifies the three times Peter denied Jesus before the crucifixion but shows the methodology of Robert Morris as the leader tending to his sheep and how they grow so fast.

After asking Peter if he loved him three times here is where the conversation goes:

In conversation one Jesus says, **"Feed my lambs."**

In conversation two Jesus says to Peter, **"Tend my sheep."**

In conversation three Jesus says, **"Feed my sheep."**

The key to growth of any organization is this:

Understand that healthy people grow. The leader's job is to "feed the sheep." So what does that really mean for you in your work?

You, the leader, have accumulated an aptitude of knowledge, skills, desire, and confidence. The "lambs and the sheep" desperately need these four things from their leader in a consistent manner to become "healthy" and grow. They need to be fed. The lambs are not as mature and need a different kind of coaching and attention than the sheep but your message and tactics must reach all of them. This is why we teach the "Whole Person" theory to growth so we are seeking to tap into all four parts of a person's nature in body (skill), mind (knowledge), heart (desire/passion), and spirit (confidence/faith). Most spend too much time on the body (skills) but never dip into the other most important parts of a person's nature (mind, heart, and spirit). This leaves a person unfulfilled and fragmented when it comes to growth.

Tangible outcomes of "feeding your sheep" means effective on-boarding which is a systematic way in which you start the relationship off by providing training so your staff can win. This includes weekly coaching and teaching, mid-week huddles, and end of week reviews. It means more than ONE performance review per year. It means you are an active participant in the growth and development of your staff and their needs. It means you are spending time with your people regularly.

Ask yourself how much time are you spending "feeding your sheep" and whether you should increase the time you spend with your people? When I ask employees what they want from their manager or leader, they all say the same thing: more of their time. Your staff is incredibly eager to spend time with you, as their yearning is to grow, to learn, to connect, and to be dynamic. The manager needs to be the coach and a mentor who is constantly finding and filling their missing structures and helping to elevate their career.

Would your people run through the wall for you because of the investment you have made in them? On the other hand, do you have an adversarial relationship with them that creates friction, burnout or even opposition within your own walls?

Always remember, "A house divided against itself shall not stand."

How Coachable are YOU?

What does coachability really mean? I frequently hear, "Well, my people are just not coachable." To me, this means:

- ▶ You've got the wrong people on the bus.
- ▶ They don't see you as a coach because you've never actually positioned yourself as a coach.
- ▶ You don't have a "coaching culture."
- ▶ You didn't set expectations when your hired staff that they were REQUIRED to learn, grow, advance, and contribute to the team, not just, or slow down the entire unit with their outdated mind-sets.

In rare instances, some people cannot be coached. Earlier, I described the three types of people who did not need coaching and how pride affects everyone, especially those who are very talented and gifted. People who feel they are very capable and have already been successful begin to believe their own hype. They insulate themselves from the "must-haves" that everybody else has to do because they are above the rules. This begins to build resentment in multiple dimensions, from the other team members and especially from the coach. Being a good teammate is hard. It requires sacrifice. It requires constantly thinking about the well-being of the team and the vision. It requires stepping aside and giving credit to others. It requires humility and recognition that you are only one part of the unit.

Remember, in a team, the strengths of some compensate for the weaknesses of others and a team's strength is when the whole is much better than the sum of its parts.

What I have not specifically addressed in this book is a serious subject. There is a lack of attention in schools to learning how to be part of a team, remaining humble when you have success, and taking coaching seriously. Our school systems do not teach you:

- ▶ How to find your talents.
- ▶ How to build, maintain, or protect your confidence.
- ▶ How to bounce back when you've been knocked down.
- ▶ How to handle coaching and respond positively to it versus shutting down.
- ▶ How to find, package, or sell your special.
- ▶ How to be a great teammate.
- ▶ How to remain coachable when you are having success.

These skills are essential in order to be a valuable and productive member of a team but there is little or no formal education training for these skills. This is particularly disappointing given that working as part of a team applies to just about every aspect of life in every corner of the globe.

You (coaches and parents) need to teach your kids from an early age the following:

1. Ability to find your "voice" or talents and bring that voice to the unit.
2. Consistency in thought, action, and follow-through.
3. Ability to admit publicly when you drop the ball or make a mistake.
4. Ability to blend your talents with others and not hog the spotlight.
5. Ability to recognize and praise every person's contribution.
6. Ability to "include" everyone to show you care about them.
7. Ability to avoid bringing outside drama inside the circle.
8. Ability to block out the noise of the world and focus on the game.

When my team was in the running for a championship, the first ever for the school, I wanted a visual to illustrate the steps it would take to win the whole thing. I pulled out all the stops, including bringing in championship rings for the players to wear, picturing the night we would win the championship, and designing a large image of the 10 steps it would take for us to be successful. Each step had a theme and each step had a story.

Finding the Right Coach for YOU

At various points in my life, I've needed different things and consequently searched out different kinds of coaches. My first business coach taught me how to sell, how to grow a small business into a large one, and how to hit my dominant aspiration by breaking it down. I've hired enterprise coaches to teach me how to scale a business, writing coaches on how to write better, financial coaches on how to invest my money for the future and more. The point is that you may need a coach who specializes in exactly what you want to do. This book has been about my coaching you to find the common missing structures associated with the growth of your business and of your life. I believe finding the right coach for you is vital. Until people buy into the messenger they will never buy into the message.

Phil Jackson and star NBA forward Dennis Rodman sat on the porch for more than three hours without saying a word when they first met at Jackson's Montana cabin. At the end of this period, they looked at each other and said, "This is the best conversation I've ever had." They could feel each other's energy. They knew they would be the right fit for each other. They believed it in their soul. Phil allowed Dennis to be the highest manifestation of him while also convincing him to be a part of the greater whole. He didn't try to change him, but rather embraced who he was and leveraged those talents within the context of the group.

Recently, I was making a pitch at a $2 billion bank in Chicago and at the very end I said, "You are probably wondering what my first move is to increase your sales by 43%, aren't you?" They all looked around the room and said, "Yes." I then said, "Well, I know one thing for sure. If your staff doesn't buy into the coach, they will never buy into his methodology."

My first move is always to get the team to buy in to me. Without this, nothing matters. Most new leaders make this mistake. They walk in, feeling confident as the new sheriff in town who is going to clean this mess up. They yell platitudes, they get too passionate about their own methodology, and they don't listen or get buy-in from the very people they need to produce. Remember the geese laying the golden eggs theory? Your people are those geese. The more they will work for you, the more golden eggs they will produce as a unit. If they don't buy in to you, then it will never work.

I understand that you may still be skeptical about why you need a coach. However, it is exactly because you do not know what you need, that you DO NEED A COACH. You need a person who has the experience, knowledge, and skill sets to find and fill your missing structures. You need a person in your life who will help you avoid the vicious cycle we've repeated in this book of good intentions, failure to follow through, and ensuing guilt. You need someone who will call you on your fluff and make sure you are doing what you are supposed to be doing. What you do not need is a "yes man." What you do not need is to shy from someone who will make you uncomfortable. I see many people say to me, "Well, I didn't like his coaching style" or, "I didn't like this or that." I bet there were things about you that they didn't like either but they still chose to pour their time, energy, creativity, and resources into you. It is not always about what you "like or don't like." It is about results. It is about a relationship with another person who can help you achieve something you could never achieve on your own. It is about driving your serious potential and it is about eliminating the emotional taxes that are costing you the big games of your life.

Here are some questions for you to answer as it relates to finding the right coach for you.

1. What is my biggest missing structure that I want to fill?
2. Do I need a strategist, a life coach, or a business coach?
3. Do I need clarity or strategy?
4. Do I need someone to vent to about my business or someone who tells me what to do?
5. Do I need someone to coach me in sales growth, marketing, or systems?
6. Do I need to bring someone in to coach and develop the talent I have acquired?
7. What am I not happy with that I feel like I need coaching in?

With the launch of this book, I've been looking for a certain kind of coach, one that specializes in successful book launches. I've also been looking for coaches who can help me go from "baby star to big star" meaning they help me elevate and amplify my brand. See how I am very specific about what kind of coach I need. You may need someone to help you grow or someone to help protect your confidence. You may need systems or structures. You may need a coach who has been there and done that and can tell you how to do it or you may need an outsider, a fresh set of eyes to look at your life and business. Here is the main thing; you need somebody who is skilled at helping other break through his or her current ceilings of complexity and get to the next level. Going at this alone is a poor decision.

You Need an OUTSIDER vs. an INSIDER

In many industries, I consider myself an outsider. I do not sell real estate although I coach thousands of real estate agents. I don't make mortgage loans although I coach thousands of mortgage originators. I don't sell insurance although I coach some of the top insurance agents and brokers in the world. You see, I have embraced the concept of being an outsider. You want me looking at your business from the outside. You want me asking the question, "If I wouldn't do business with you, then why not?" You want me working with other top people so I can tell you what the best people in the world are doing. You want a fresh pair of eyes looking at something toward which you are biased. Remember the saying, "You can't see the picture when you are inside the frame?" I call this "The Seinfeld Phenomenon."

When the writers of *Seinfeld* pitched their show to the networks, they brought in focus groups and comedy writers to see whether it would be a fit, a common practice at networks to decide whether to "green-light" the program. In both the focus groups and with the comedy writers, *Seinfeld* scored very low, so low that the network couldn't see how it could run the program. The executives drank the comedy Kool-Aid and had what's called a false negative, meaning they thought something was wrong, primarily because they were too close to the action. They watched and wrote comedy all day every day. Enter Rick Ludwin.

Ludwin didn't work in the comedy department; he handled variety and specials. When *Seinfeld* failed to pilot, Ludwin stepped in and tried to revive it. He pledged to find time in the somewhere in the lineup to insert this show. The network only ordered four episodes, a very small number. Ludwin's fresh eyes saw the potential of *Seinfeld*. It was Ludwin who didn't drink the comedy Kool-Aid and forcefully said the show would work. To say it worked would be a major understatement. *Seinfeld* would go on to gross more than $1 BILLION in revenue as one of the most successful TV programs ever. This success would never have happened if the so-called comedy experts had their say.

I see this same concept in book publishing. How many times did *Harry Potter, Rich Dad Poor Dad, The 4-Hour Workweek* or *Chicken Soup for the Soul* get rejected? Editors look at manuscripts every day and sometimes they miss out on books that become some of the best sellers of all time.

I'm able to see your business with fresh eyes. I don't drink the Kool-Aid every day. I can see the missing structures clearly even when you cannot. You need an OUTSIDER looking at your business. You need a skeptic on your board of directors. You need a naysayer to step in when you are blinded by your own passion for your projects. You need a coach who will tell you the truth versus tell you what you want to hear.

Earlier in the book, we talked about bias, assumption, and prejudice. This is where you bring a skewed opinion toward your own work. I believe that we all deeply overvalue our own contribution to any equation. I believe that you should be asking those you lead or those you serve how well you meet their needs. I believe you need to travel and study various industries and cultures to become truly great. Steve Jobs spent time in India before forming Apple. Many of the greatest designers lived in other countries, taking in other cultures for extended periods. And most of the greats "combine" past vocations and occupations into their work to bring something NEW to the game as I did when I combined sports and business to o inner-engineer my players from the inside out.

The outsider approach is valuable but many organizations stick to tried and true and hire people who have stuck to the same formula no longer works. Have you ever noticed how an NBA coach who gets fired quickly gets another job, only to lose that as well? The teams recycle losers but what they need is an outsider, not an insider, to look at their organization. They need new ideas, freshness, and life. They need to quit "living with the dead."

Why don't people bring insiders in? Bias, assumption, and prejudgment. They have already made up their mind that an outside person cannot be valuable to them. You will be making this costly mistake if you don't get feedback from two important groups: your consumers and your outsiders.

Legacy Building

I want to end this book talking about legacy. I want you to build an organization that will be around 100 years from now. I want your name carved in history as a person who left a significant mark on the world. I want you to drive a legacy for your family through the deep contributions that you make. I want your imprint to be as prominent as that of the Rockefellers, J.P. Morgan, Cornelius Vanderbilt, Henry Ford, and Thomas Edison.

When I look back over my coaching career there is one thing of which I am most proud. It wasn't the championship that we won, although I'll never forget that night. It was what we built. After I left athletic coaching at age 31, the team that I led for nine years as a head coach and three as an assistant would go on to achieve even more success. The program didn't wither away; my team would go on to win four more championships, totaling five in a seven-year cycle. The team went on to become the #1 team in the country, not just in the South.

That is what I want you to build. I want you to build something that you will know was worth all your effort and sacrifice. You should be able to sit back and say that all your worth was worth it. You helped create "something special." I lay awake at night now thinking of how I can build a "must-have" in the world instead of something "nice to have."

For me it looks like "The Greatness Factory," a unique destination for people who have made a decision to be great. It is where teams can gather, salespeople can sharpen their skills, managers can transition to becoming coaches, and ordinary people can become "People of Interest." This Factory will be located in every state so people can get the skills they need at an affordable price. There will be courses in sales, leadership, personal branding, building teams, and scaling a company. Whether you attend a 45-minute session or weeks of coaching, you will be transformed and inspired. I still believe in live training. I still believe in seeing the concert live, not just listening to a CD. I still believe that we need to associate and spend time with like-minded people who want more—and more does not always mean more money. It means more confidence, more structure, more freedom, more impact, and more of life

I still believe in the activation of potential and I believe we can build something that never goes away, and always affects people around the world. I still believe in building something that my four-year-old daughter can eventually run and the pass down to her children. I still believe in legacy. Proverbs 13:23 tells us that, "A good person leaves an inheritance for his children's children." Think about what you will be passing on?

THE FUTURE OF COACHING

While traveling back from a speaking engagement I had to drive through my hometown of Woodbury, Tennessee. I was up early and traveling and didn't get a chance to eat breakfast, so I stopped at the famous Joe's Place on the Square. I was waited on by a young girl just out of high school. She had a pleasant attitude and smiled. She was very pretty and friendly but seemed to have little or no direction in her life. She stumbled around, lost her confidence when people got on her, and tried to remember what little training she had. *However, I could see something in this young girl.* I could see her potential. I could sense that she had latent talent that she had no idea she had. While checking out I asked her, "Is there a reason you chose this work?" She responded, "Well, my mother bakes the pies here and they asked her one day if I would be willing to be a server because they needed one." Even they saw the good in her too.

That young woman may flounder around for some time in her life and live off her looks, personality, and smile. This will get her somewhere but **the traits she displayed that day are** what are called "secondary greatness" or "personality traits." She may

167

never dig into her "primary greatness," which is her God-given abilities that were placed in her while she was still in her mother's womb. These talents will have to be uncovered, and nurtured and most likely it will take the help of an expert to help her see and reach her potential. Without a coach, she only has a 50/50 chance, if that, to find her real calling in life.

I grew up in that same small town. *I survived on personality.* I did not find my primary greatness until coaches walked into my life, took an interest in me and helped me to find my voice, and ultimately encouraged me to help others find their voices. ***I believe God placed coaches in the world because he knew that left to our own devices we will never dig down deep and see the "Acres of Diamonds" we were sitting on.*** The coach affirms and validates the worth and potential in people in so clear a way that they begin to see it in themselves. The coach shares insights and strategies that elevate and accelerate that potential. Without the coach, we would be left going down the path on which we're traveling…and usually we would not get to where we should, on our own.

The future of coaching is changing. I predict that within the next five years every manager will become a coach skilled at maximizing and honing the talents and gifts of their human capital. They will have to teach differentiation, invention and creativity, and competitive intelligence. They will have to become world-class at recruiting and attracting better talent, coaching and developing that talent, and retaining that talent. Coaching goes beyond being a manager. As a coach, you lead people. You inspire people. You motivate people. A manager handles processes, numbers, and systems, which do not have a body, mind, heart, or spirit.

There will be more and more coaches in both the athletic and business arena. Although they will never replace in-person coaching, online and virtual coaching will also become more commonplace given the advances in technology and the rapid pace of life today. I predict that athletic coaches will make the great crossover to being business savvy Coach-epreneurs who know how to run organizations, how to market and sell, and how to get and keep the attention of the world. They will no longer just be able to get by on Xs and Os. They will have to understand and tap into the Whole Person and motivate the body, the mind, the heart, and the spirit, or they will quickly become obsolete.

I predict that we will continue to see high achievers who want a competitive advantage turn to an expert regardless of their skill level. These major producers are enlightened enough to recognize they need a skilled professional guiding, correcting, and holding them accountable so they can achieve peak performance levels.

I predict that the two buzzwords of the year in organizations will be "culture and accountability." Leaders want to build cultures that embrace the potential of their staff but don't know how. Most cultures are lazy, apathetic, and dated. There is no life. There is no energy. There is no expectation. There is no excitement. However, great coaches can walk into those organizations and turn them around. The coaches have the guts to have the hard conversations with the underperformers. The coaches will say to the CEO of a $250 million company, "If you just solved these three problems your revenue could exceed $1 billion per year." The coaches will inspire the youth of America and pull inner city kids out of drugs and poverty and show them that through and with their God-given talents they and their families can have a better life.

As I reflect on my athletic coaching career, I'm always amazed at how much time I actually spent with my players. Out of the 80 hours per week that I worked, 70 of those hours were spent in thinking, strategizing, and actual contact coaching time with my team. It consumed my life. I poured all of my heart and soul into my team. On average, I spent more than five hours per day with my players. Per week, that was more than 27.5 hours into the player; per month, that is 110 hours; and per year, more than 1,320 hours into each person. This comes to more than **5,280** hours over a four-year period.

How much influence and impact can someone have when he spends more than a thousand hours per year with each person? Most people get 15 minutes per week with a manager. How much transformation can really take place in 15 minutes? The game of coaching for many has become "transactional versus transformational." *You can't transform another person's life in 15 minutes per week.* You can't even learn much someone in that limited time.

Why don't more people coach in today's world? It takes an incredible amount of time and energy to pour into another person on whom you may or may not get a return. It takes an incredible amount of time and energy to "slow down" to "speed up." It takes noticing, caring, correcting, rebuking, and celebrating to be a good coach. Coaching requires a selfless approach. It takes thinking and spending time with another person to change his life. It takes reading, studying, and practicing. In addition, many people can't balance helping other children and parents when they have their own families. Coaching is emotionally taxing.

I firmly believe that one of the most underappreciated group of people in the world is the coaches. When I speak around the country and ask, "How many of you have ever had a great coach?" you should see how many hands go up. You should see the smiles that emerge on people's faces. I then ask, "Is it true that when you had that great coach in your life that you experienced the most growth you ever have had in your life? They all say, "Yes." Most of us got to where we are today because another person looked at us and said, "I believe in you" and "You can do this." Without those people we don't take steps in the direction of our dreams, we don't overcome our lack of faith and confidence, and we don't become what we are capable of becoming. Without them, we fail to sing the song we were meant to sing. We should take the time to say thank you to those coaches who have changed our life.

I will end this book the way it began. *I believe you have a song to sing and there is an audience waiting to hear to it. I also believe a good coach can change your life.*

The question remains, "Will you be coachable," and if you are a coach, "Will you become a coach for whom people would be excited to play?"

If not, something has to change on both sides of this equation.

Very few people ever say, "I would run through the wall for my manager," but they do say, "I would run through the wall for my coach."

ABOUT THE AUTHOR

Micheal Burt is *The Super Coach*, who blends a unique focus and intensity with an entrepreneurial mind-set. He started coaching at age 15 and spent the first decade of his professional life winning championships as a head women's basketball coach. He infuses business principles into the athletic world and athletic principles into the business world in a way that accelerates growth and gets serious results. He is the go-to expert in the country with a unique ability to coach groups and individuals toward a dominant and important goal. He takes the complicated and makes it simple. This unique blend of sports and business experience along with his ability to extract, synthesize, and share concepts that EVERY person can understand make him an asset for people who aspire to find their voice, activate their talents, and break through their past ceilings to reach greater success.

Coach Burt has been hired by some of the biggest brands in the world to "coach up" their people including Dell, INC., Ohio National, Coldwell Banker, Century 21, National Health Care, Vanderbilt University, Invest Financial Corporation, Investors Bank, Better Homes and Gardens Real Estate, and others.

Coach Burt is also the host of *The Super Coach Show*, a weekly online TV show and podcast that seeks to multiply your life, your money, and your business and help you find the Achilles heel that is holding you back. You can follow Coach Burt, watch his shows, and more at www.coachburt.com. Coach Burt is the founder of *The Greatness Factory*, a unique destination location that "takes people from all walks of life and manufactures greatness." See more about the coaching and training programs at www.mygreatnessfactory.com.

Everybody Needs a Coach in Life is Coach Burt's eleventh book. He also speaks more than 150 times nationally every year and practices what he preaches, regularly coaching teams and individuals as a practitioner.

Previous books:

Changing Lives through Coaching
The Inspirational Leader
This Ain't No Practice Life
The Anatomy of Winning
Success Simplified
Zebras and Cheetahs
Person of Interest